Pagan Kennedy's

LiVING

A Handbook for Maturing Hipsters

sfwp.com

To my mom—

living proof that there's nothing hipper than maturity

Acknowledgments

Thanks to everyone who consented to be interviewed and photographed for this book, allowing me to delve into their nontraditional lives. Scot Hacker and Sprax Lines came to my rescue whenever my cranky PC crashed. My writers group—Lauren Slater, Karen Propp, Nadine Boughton, and Mary Clark—Helped edit the essays and even the cartoons. Sprax and Marcus Aurin frequently acted as photographers, and I borrowed all kinds of equipment from Sprax and Scot. As always, my friends came up with many of the ideas in here. I just happened to be the one to write them down.

Find Pagan online at www.pagankennedyproject.com and www.pagankennedy.net

Library of Congress Cataloging-in-Publication Data

Kennedy, Pagan, 1962-
Pagan Kennedy's living : the handbook for maturing hipsters.
        pages cm
Originally published: New York : St. Martin's Griffin, 1997.
Includes bibliographical references and index.
ISBN 978-1-939650-50-4 (trade pbk. : alk. paper)
1. Lifestyles—United States. 2. Hippies—United States. I. Title. II. Title: Living.
HQ2044.U6K45 2015
305.5'68—dc23
                                2015026209

Published by SFWP
369 Montezuma Ave. #350
Santa Fe, NM 87501
(505) 428-9045
www.sfwp.com

Pagan Kennedy's
LIVING

Also by Pagan Kennedy

★ PLATFORMS:
A Microwaved Cultural Chronicle of
the 1970s

★ SPINSTERS

★ STRIPPING
and Other Stories

★ ZINE:
How I Spent Six Years of My Life in
the Underground and Finally Found
Myself...I Think

★ THE DANGEROUS JOY OF DR. SEX
and Other True Stories

★ BLACK LIVINGSTONE

★ THE FIRST MAN-MADE MAN

★ EXES

★ CONFESSIONS OF A MEMORY EATER

★ INVENTOLOGY

★ CONTENTS ★

manifesto orama

You're an aging slacker. In fact, you've been slacking off for so long that you can hardly remember what it was you originally decided to slack off from. Years ago, you left the mainstream world of career paths, malls, expensive hair-care products, regular TV viewing, and wearing deodorant. Instead, you've taken up residence in this strange place at the edge of town, where the frozen-yogurt boutiques yield to thrift shops, where the mailboxes on the triple-deckers are covered with scratched-out names, where the jukebox in the diner sill knows how to play "Gypsies, Tramps, and Thieves."

You wouldn't live anywhere else. You've grown to love this part of town. But there is one niggling problem. You've begun to notice that, while this is the perfect place to be young, it's a hard place to be, well, not so young. You never quite feel settled here. Everyone keeps moving around—people are always trading apartments, roommates, bandmates, jobs, girlfriends and boyfriends. Your life sometimes feels like the Mad Hatter's Tea Party; you have to keep switching your seat, and you never know what kind of odd characters will share the table with you.

Yet in the midst of this chaos, you've managed to build a family out of housemates, co-workers, neighbors, lovers, ex-lovers, and ex-lover's ex-lovers. There's often someone sleeping on your couch. Whenever you clean out your pantry, you find strange plates and dishes and you're not sure which roommate or boyfriend/ girlfriend left them there. You've accumulated a pile of other peoples' keys—to apartments, to cars, to motorcycles, to practice rooms. This revolving-door community was fine when you were in your early twenties, but could you carry on a really, really long-term monogamous relationship in the midst of this chaos? Would you want to? And how do you raise kids on this side of town?

Then there's the job thing. Most likely, you've learned how to earn a living without losing your human dignity—and that's required some compromises. Maybe you work part-time and do your art on the side, in which case you make ends meet by living like a monk. Maybe at this point you've actually decided to become a monk—after all, you might get paid to sit on your butt all day and you wouldn't have to do data entry. Or maybe you've found a job you love, but it pays a pittance and your funding is always about to be out. Maybe you're stuck in some white-collar job that bores you, but instead of quitting you've decided to Quit in Place— you pretend to do your work, all the while using the office's phones, faxes, and copy machines for your own illicit purposes. Maybe you've become a professional temp or freelancer. Whatever your job situation, if you live on the slacking side of town, you probably don't have any health insurance, savings, or security. At this rate, it looks like you may spend your retirement years in a house with five roommates and some stained futon furniture.

But wait! Don't lose hope. I know there's a lot of pressure to sign up for The Program—get a full-time job, buy a car on credit, move to the suburbs, get married, stop doing your art. Actually, there's a lot to be said for The Program: It's a clear-cut path through the wilderness, a path that

don't lose hope

leads a lot of people to happiness. And those of us who can get with The Program any time we want should never forget how lucky we are. For much of the world, these banal American luxuries are not even an option. But just because we can have gas-guzzling cars, pointless desk jobs, and wall-to-wall carpeting, should we?

A lot of people are quietly pioneering a different kind of life for themselves. They're patching together bizarre families, inventing new types of romantic relationships to suit their needs, finding low-budget and creative ways to raise their kids, tuning out the mainstream media, doing what they love, and trusting that the money will follow.

How do you know whether you yourself are one of the pioneers? Here's the test: When you meet someone at a party and they ask you what you do, can you sum up your job in a few words or does it take you half an hour to adequately explain your situation? Same goes for living arrangements. If your life is incredibly complex and jury-rigged, consider yourself a success. You have managed to resist The Program. Of course, if you can't pass the fifteen-word test, well, that can be okay, too. You may have accepted society's labels even while subverting them. The important thing

manifesto orama

is to live your own life—not the life that's being sold to you by a bunch of corporations.

Designing your own job or family unit or living situation from the ground up takes a lot of energy, especially in these dark days when anyone tainted by non-traditionalism gets lynched by the media. Marcia Clark, Joycelyn Elders, Patricia Ireland—such women have been vilified as Bad Moms, Masturbation Fiends, and Bisexual Good-for-Nothings when in fact they are just sensible people trying to pursue happiness without hurting anyone.

why are those women so dangerous?

Why are those women so dangerous? Why are the Powers That Be attacking anyone who doesn't imitate Ward or June Cleaver? There can only be one answer: Lifestyle choices are the front lines of the political battle these days. And if we consumers fail to live the way Corporate America wishes us to, we become dangerous. When we form our own communities, when we find our furniture in the trash, when we take care of our friends who can't take care of themselves, when we organize our own old-age homes and day-care centers, when we make our own fun, when we refuse to drive cars, when we turn off our TVs, when we do all that and more, well then, Corporate America has little to sell to us. We might not need Exxon, General Electric, or Procter & Gamble. We probably wouldn't need full-time jobs. And we certainly wouldn't need products like L'Oreal ("because I'm worth it") to make us feel important.

The first step toward that utopia is for us alternative types to find one another and share information about how to live graciously on this side of town. If you want to learn how to serve pumpkin consommé in hollowed-out pumpkin shells, then read *Martha Stewart's Living*. But if you'd rather score some pumpkins for free from the supermarket trash and then make soup to feed your sixteen housemates, two dogs, and three lovers, and then turn the shells into an alternative energy source, well, *Pagan Kennedy's Living* is the place for you.

Okay, I'm done being self-righteous. On to the fun part...

MYSTERY DATES

When I was a kid, I owned a game called Mystery Date. The goal was to move around the board, collecting the handbags and hats you would need for, say, a skiing date or a black-tie affair. Then you got a chance to spin the handle of a miniature plastic door and open it up to find out who your "date" would be. Depending on where the latch caught, the door would open to reveal a ski instructor, a guy dressed up for the prom, these two other guys I can't remember at all, or a bum. If you got the bum, you lost the game.

Mystery Date taught me that if I wanted to live a sensible and serene life, I should pick a partner who matched my shoes and hat. The thing is, I don't want to live a sensible or serene life—nor do any of my friends. Maybe that's why everyone I know who played that game when they were kids—women and gay men alike—lusted after the bum. Accessories be damned: We all knew that the bum, with his stubble and his cigar and his dirty pants, would show us a really good time.

When I was a kid, I thought that I'd grow up and go on dates with clean-cut guys wearing color-coordinated outfits; I'd be polite to them, but always turn down their proposals of marriage. I would wait for a bum to appear at my door, and when he did, I'd stick an old stogey in my mouth, jump in his jalopy, and ride away with him to a life of adventure. Unfortunately, Mystery Date didn't prepare me—didn't prepare any of us—for love in the nineties. Because these days there are just so many bums to choose from, of so many different persuasions. Gay, straight, bi, femme, butch, nancy boy, macho, transvestite, pierced, not pierced, on medication, not on medication—how do you know which one is right for you? How do you even know that one person is right for you? The average American marriage lasts about seven years (according to recent census statistics), so maybe most of us are designed to live with a series of partners. Or maybe you're happy being single.

One thing is sure: None of us can expect to fling open a door and find love. We've got to make it happen.

A new phenomenon of the nineties...

MEN WHO WON'T PUT OUT

CASE STUDY #1: LENNY

MY FRIEND MARIA RELATES...

I MET LENNY WHEN I WAS VERY DOWN. DON'T ASK. HE WAS DEPRESSED TOO SINCE HE'D JUST LOST HIS JOB. ON OUR FIRST DATE, WE WENT TO SEE BERGMAN'S "CRIES AND WHISPERS," WHICH SET THE TONE FOR ALL THAT FOLLOWED.

IS LIFE REALLY AS PAINFUL AND HOPELESS AS IN THAT MOVIE?

OH GOD, MARIA, I'VE BEEN SITTING IN MY HOUSE TRYING TO WRITE COVER LETTERS BUT I CAN'T EVEN GET PAST THE "DEAR SIR."

NEXT DATE...

CINEMA
TONITE:
LADY & THE TRAMP

TWO PLEASE.

I'M REALLY GLAD WE DID SOMETHING LIGHTWEIGHT. THIS REALLY CHEERED ME UP.

I HAVEN'T MET ANYONE LIKE YOU IN A LONG TIME, MARIA. SOMEONE I REALLY CLICK WITH.

THIS IS GREAT. I DON'T FEEL AWKWARD AT ALL. SHOULD I STICK MY TONGUE IN HIS MOUTH?

NEXT DAY

SO, MARIA, TELL ME THE DAY AND TIME YOU WERE BORN SO I CAN PUT THEM INTO MY COMPUTER AND CHECK OUR ASTROLOGICAL COMPATIBILITY...

WHEN I SEE THIS GUY TOMORROW, I'M GOING TO JUMP HIS BONES.

SOON

SLURP

SMACK

PANT

PANT

OH JESUS. WHAT HAPPENED? WHERE AM I?

LET'S DRIVE OUT TO THE BEACH. LET'S GO AWAY FOR THE WHOLE WEEKEND!

WAIT. NO. I NEED SOME TIME ALONE NOW. I JUST DO. OK?

LOOK, LENNY, I'M SORRY I FREAKED OUT THIS MORNING. I'M FEELING A LOT BETTER NOW.

IT'S OK. YOU KNOW WHEN I WALKED AWAY FROM YOUR APARTMENT, I HAD THE FEELING THAT WE'D JUST BE FRIENDS AFTER THIS. GOOD FRIENDS...

GEEZ, THAT WAS FAST. THE WORST PART IS, I CAN'T FIGURE OUT WHO DUMPED WHO.

ANYWAY, IT'S A GOOD EXCUSE TO START SMOKING AGAIN. I DESERVE A CIGARETTE AFTER THAT.

MEN WHO WON'T PUT OUT

MY FRIEND GINA RELATES...

EDDIE'S 39, SMART, AND HANDSOME IN AN ERIC CLAPTON WAY. WHEN I MET HIM, HE'D JUST BROKEN OFF A THREE-YEAR RELATIONSHIP WITH A WOMAN WHO WAS 21. GO AHEAD, DO THE MATH. THAT'S RIGHT, SHE WAS 18 WHEN THEY STARTED GOING OUT.

GLOBAL VILLAGE PEOPLE

CASE STUDY #2: EDDIE

FOR FOUR DATES, WE DIDN'T EVEN TOUCH, BUT IT WAS STILL VERY SEXY.

YOU'RE MUCH CUTER THAN GRETA GARBO. SHE'S TOO HARSH LOOKING, DON'T YOU THINK?

UM, SURE. I CAN LIVE WITH BEING CUTER THAN GRETA GARBO.

READERS:

THESE TWO STORIES REPRESENT DOZENS OF OTHERS THAT HAVE BEEN TOLD TO ME AT BRIDAL SHOWERS AND OVER THE PHONE. WHY HAVEN'T *TIME* AND *NEWSWEEK*, THOSE STAUNCH BASTIONS OF LIFESTYLE REPORTING, PICKED UP ON THIS STORY? MEN NOT PUTTING OUT SEEMS TO BE THE SILENT EPIDEMIC OF THE NINETIES. THE WOMEN WHO HAVE TOLD ME THESE STORIES ARE BRAINY INDEPENDENT BABES WHO'VE PROVED THEMSELVES CAPABLE OF LONG-TERM COMMITMENT—SO DON'T BLAME THE VICTIMS, OK? SOMETHING IS TERRIBLY WRONG. AND THAT'S WHY I'M CALLING ON A PANEL OF NOTABLE FEMINISTS TO COMMENT…

Some of America's Most Visible Female Pundits Comment on the Men Who Don't Put Out

(But they didn't really say any of this, okay?)

MEN ARE AFRAID OF INDEPENDENT, SEXUALLY LIBERATED WOMEN BECAUSE THE MEDIA TEACHES THEM TO BE. LOOK AT "FATAL ATTRACTION." A MAN HAS CASUAL SEX WITH A SINGLE WOMAN AND SHE TURNS INTO A PSYCHOKILLER WHO GOES AFTER HIS WIFE. NO WONDER MEN ARE AFRAID. THE MEDIA PORTRAYS SINGLE WOMEN AS DESPERATE TO TRAP MEN..... WHEREAS IN REAL LIFE (ACCORDING TO ONE STUDY) SINGLE WOMEN ARE HAPPIER THAN MARRIED WOMEN.

SUSAN FALUDI

ALL HETEROSEXUAL INTERCOURSE IS A FORM OF RAPE. THE MEN WHO WON'T PUT OUT ARE HEROES. THEY'RE TRYING NOT TO PERPETUATE A SYSTEM THEY KNOW IS WRONG. THEY'RE BEHAVING AS DECENTLY AS POSSIBLE FOR MEMBERS OF A GENDER THAT IS INHERENTLY SICK AND DEPRAVED AND PHYSICALLY EQUIPPED FOR A VIOLENT ACT OF PENETRATION.

ANDREA DWORKIN

THESE WOMEN MIGHT NOT IDENTIFY THEMSELVES AS FEMINISTS PER SE, EVEN THOUGH THEY ARE GRAPPLING WITH POLITICAL ISSUES OF SEX AND POWER. WOMEN, AS A GROUP, HAVE TO DEAL WITH THE FACT THAT MANY MEN STILL WANT TO CONTROL SEX. THIS ISSUE IS MOST DIFFICULT FOR THOSE OF US WHO HAPPEN TO BE TOTAL BABES.

NAOMI WOLF

WHY'D YOU PUT ME IN WITH THESE FEMINIST LOSERS? THEY'RE THE REASON MEN WON'T PUT OUT! LOOK, SEX IS A BRUTAL ACT, BUT THESE FEMINIST PRICKS WANT TO PRETEND THAT IT'S SOME KIND OF P.C. ROMP THROUGH THE TULIPS! GEEZ. BY THE WAY, DID YOU KNOW I WATCH TEN TV SETS AT ONCE?

CAMILLE PAGLIA

why bring me into this? why should i care about the neuroses of a bunch of white, probably middle-class het.s? now as i was saying, cultural imperialism ...

bell hooks

As you enter your late twenties, or perhaps your thirties, dating becomes much more complicated than it used to be. Now everyone you meet has an extensive track record. And so do you.

Therefore, when you meet with a prospective partner, you may find yourself acting as if you're on a job interview instead of a date. You carefully slip in references to past boyfriends/girlfriends to prove that you have many credentials in the field of relationship-ology. You casually refer to your mature and committed behavior during those previous entanglements.

Meanwhile, as your date natters on about his/her life, you listen for those chance remarks that will help clue you in to his/her emotional health. Was he/she capable of living with an enamorata, and if so, did he/she do the dishes?

Well, we at Pagan Kennedy's Living have a suggestion. Stop pussyfooting around. Make yourself a Relationship Résumé and hand it out to all your prospective mates.

Herewith, we include the beginning of a sample résumé to get you started.

Relationship Résumé

JOHN DOE
12 Larkspur Lane
Yourtown, U.S.A. 12345

OBJECTIVE

A casual tumble in the hay, possibly leading up to a long-term position.

EDUCATION

Junior High—Frequent pot smoker in woods behind school. Listened in on many conversations concerning human sexuality.

High School—Went out with Debbie Rafferty for two years, culminating in intercourse and prom attendance. Extended flirtation with Linda Goldman, leading to lab partnership.

College—Participated in numerous binges, during which techniques were honed. Year-long dalliance with French exchange student; developed language skills.

Post-Collegiate—Three-year, semi-long-distance relationship with Laura Marks. Proved ability to be effective communicator over the phone.

Two years living with Sarah Smith. Duties included taking out trash, checking closet for spiders, making pots of tea, dividing bills. Relationship required impressive sexual performance, abilities as a self-starter, willingness to travel, and ability to adjust to fast-paced environment in a growing field.

Suckdog Speaks...

...about getting sex through the mail

Here's an interview I did with Lisa Suckdog—also known as Lisa Carver—a performance artist and the mind behind an amazing zine called Rollerderby. *Lisa became famous for her willingness to jump around naked in front of an audience and to smear blood and other scary fluids on her body. She's also rumored to have run through men faster than Liz Taylor, though these days, Lisa seems to have become a one-man woman, just like in the country songs. She now lives in Denver with her boyfriend and their baby.*

How did Lisa seek out and seduce so many misfit bachelors over the years? Here she shares her secrets with all of you who like to date without leaving the comfort of your own homes.

Lisa, after two weeks of being together, you and your boyfriend decided to have a kid. Is that true?

We'd been writing and talking on the phone for a while, actually.

But had you met each other before that?

No. We wrote and talked for a month and a half. Then I went out to see him for a week, and then I went home and then I went to visit for another week and that's when we decided to have a kid.

Wow.

That's the way all my relationships are. Fast, I mean

You always have mail-order grooms?

Yeah. Because I'm a peculiar person and it's not like my next-door neighbor is going to be right for me. So every major boyfriend I've had I met through the mail.

Wow. So tell me about other mail-order relationships.

Well, the first one I had...Well the *very* first relationship I had was with this dork who worked in a furniture shop and would come in and buy coffee from me at Dunkin' Donuts. I was fifteen. And I never made that mistake again. So from then on I knew I'd have to meet them through the mail.

Then my next one—I interviewed his band in Boston— I was sixteen. The interview went well so we had sex.

You consummated it.

Yeah. I think it's good for journalism to have sex with the people you interview. They tell you a lot of things they wouldn't have otherwise. Also, if I'm interviewing someone I must think they're interesting. I want to have sex with them anyway.

So, um, how many other mail-order relationships have you had?

I think I've only had four serious relationships. And also, all the people I've had one-night stands with, they were also mail-order or I'd meet them on the road [touring with the Suckdog performance ensemble].

How do you seduce somebody through the mail?
One way is to say "I want to have sex with you." That's what I did with X [her current boyfriend]. Others you might not want to be so forward with. First you interview them. You act really complimentary and interested, just like you would in real life.

You write to them and ask to interview them?
Yeah, they fall for it every time.

So that's like the first date, the interview?
And the second date is the follow-up questions. And then you just find some excuse to meet and then you have sex.

Awright!
If you want to take your time about it you write an interesting and sexy piece about them [for some fanzine] and say how brilliant they are.

My second mail-order groom I met on the road when I was touring, and I gave him a blow job. I thought he was really cute. Actually, no, what had happened was, he interviewed me through the mail, and I'd never met him. I was busy at the time so I didn't pursue it. And then I met him and I didn't know it was him.

How embarrassing.
Well, it wasn't embarrassing because he was cute and I said, "Come here."(I was very forward for a couple of years.) I found out later he was the one who had interviewed me. So we had sex, and then I flew to France and when I called him from France he accused me of giving him a genital disease but I *had not* given him a genital disease. He just hadn't taken enough showers.

You gave him a what?
A genital disease.

Oh *genital disease*. Sorry. I can hardly hear you because I have the tape recorder stuck between my ear and the receiver. So, anyway, he got the genital disease from somebody else?
No, he just didn't bathe enough, so he was irritated down there. That argument between us brought out a lot of harsh emotions, which brought us together. So then he almost immediately came to live with me when I went back to New Hampshire. Then we were happy for a year, and miserable for a year, then we

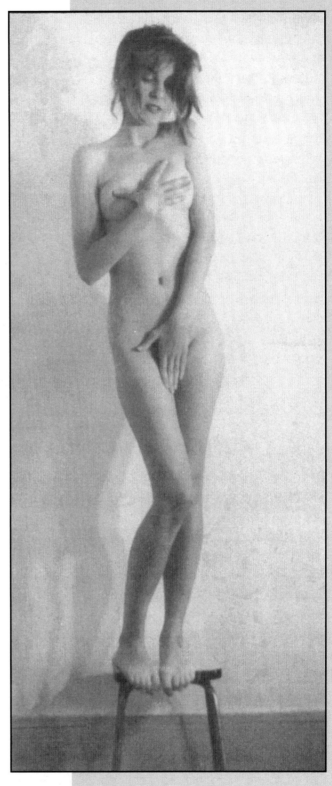

broke up and I moved to California to be with another mail-order groom, who I was miserable with after a month. So there I was, stuck in California.

Did you know this guy when you moved out there?

I'd met him, but I didn't remember him because I was drunk. I chased him down the street. That's all I know of it. But he had a girlfriend at the time. I had to drive the girlfriend away.

When you got to California?

No, I drove her away with my charming letters. I am a charming writer. I think I'm more charming in letters than in real life. In real life, I'm self-obsessed and busy. In the mail, it doesn't take much time to make charming observations about the other person and pretend they're all I think about.

You can construct the perfect self for them.

It's actually pretty fake. But that's how I get them trapped. Then I can be my real self and they're stuck with me 'cause they're in love.

If you're constructing a false self, isn't there a high chance for disappointment?

Well, that's beautiful, that falling-in-love part. And when you're mail-ordering, you can stretch that out. Or if you get really excited, you can cut it short and go visit them. You're in control of the falling in love. It's usually a lot better than the real thing.

So, falling in love—you've turned it into a sport almost.

Yeah.

But with the guy in California—that represented the downside of falling in love through the mail.

I really wouldn't consider it a downside. I had fun falling in love. And I had fun for a month. And after that it was miserable, but so what, it was an experience.

But another good thing about writing and calling before you meet someone is—I don't know about you—but if I am attracted to someone I have to have sex immediately. So the good thing about letters is that you can get totally worked up like you never could in real life, because if I see someone cute and I'm single, I have to have sex with him that night. But with these long-distance things, you can have a lot of fantasies about the person and you can even talk to them about what to do. By the time you finally meet, ohmygod, you're about to explode.

Oh, I forgot to mention! I've had five major relationships, including my husband.

Yeah, so you guys started corresponding. Who wrote who first?

I wrote him first because somebody gave me one of his tapes and I thought it was really funny. So I wrote to him and said, "I love your tape. Here's my tape." And then he wrote and said, "I love your tape. Here's a picture of me." And then I sent him a picture of me and I was naked.

You don't mess around.

I was eighteen and *hot*.

So what about with X [her current boyfriend]?

Well, at first I hated him. I wanted him dead.

It's just like in a cheesy romance story where they start out hating each other.

I was so angry I would have arguments about him.

Why did you hate him so much?

I thought he was a bad man who manipulated people. I thought he was more interested in power than the truth.

But you didn't know him.

No, I'd never met him. But he's a famous fellow, and I had read interviews with him and my roommate was infatuated with him. I told her, "You shouldn't be infatuated with people like that. He's a bad person." I'd call people up and say, "What do you think of X?" And they'd say, "I think he's a Nazi." And I'd say, "I think he is, too. I hate him." In fact, it may all be a prank. I think everybody was tired of me talking about him. And then I was in the bathtub on Thursday at 2 P.M. in September 1993 and it hit me that I was really just mad he wasn't manipulating *me*.

So then I called up my friend Rachel and told her all about it, and then I transcribed what we said and I faxed all that to him. Then I called him up and asked him what he thought, and he said, "I liked it." And that was all he said!

In my conversation with Rachel, I expressed the desire to have sex with him. But he didn't even talk about that; he talked about going up in a hot-air balloon.

I thought all he said was that he liked the fax.

He said he liked the fax and then he started talking about the hot-air balloon.

Well, he felt awkward, clearly.

No, he didn't even feel awkward. He told me later he was getting hot and cold signals from me because *I* was really scared to death. I was shaking. So he said I sounded snotty.

So then I was talking to him for hours every day on the phone, but nothing was ever said about sex. Which was weird. And yet we never mentioned it. We were talking about Olivia Newton-John, and people that we know, and people that we hate. And so I didn't know what to think. Then finally he told me he'd had a dream about me and he'd send me a letter about it. In the letter, he said we had sex in the dream. But I still didn't know for sure if he was interested.

Well, he was talking on the phone to you every day.

My roommate told me he's a friendly guy and he would talk to anybody, which is not true, but I believed her. So then we met and had drinks—and didn't have sex immediately. Well, we had sex that night, but we waited several hours.

That's very commendable.

I guess we were having fun talking.

[Lisa and I are silent for a second. Then she suddenly seems to remember something]

You know, there's some information I would like to share with you. It's not true that you become vaginally loose after you have a baby. If you do your Kegel exercises, you can be as tight as—if not more so—than you were before. I didn't used to do Kegel exercises—I thought, I'm young, I'm free. And then, when I got pregnant, I had to do fifty Kegels a day. And now I'm in the habit, so I keep on doing them.

So once again, an American self-improvement regimen saves the day.

I think you can solve any problem with hard work.

And that's it, isn't it? The Generation L platform. Stop whining and make the most of what you've got.

Exactly. Look good. Be good. Work hard. Be nice.

So, it's basically what we were taught on Romper Room.

Yeah, except there's a lot more sex to it.

The Third Sex

One night when Barb came home, the door slammed behind her with an unfamiliar echoing sound. Then she saw why: The hall rug had disappeared. She dropped her grocery bags and hurried into the living room. Books lay stacked on the floor where the shelves should have been. Her boyfriend had taken his pictures too, leaving squares of white on the sooty wall.

She lowered herself to the floor and rested her head on her knees. It occurred to her that maybe he'd thrown all of his stuff in a U-Haul and would drive up in a few hours, tell her he'd made a mistake, and together they would carry everything back into the apartment again. But she knew him too well to believe this.

After perhaps an hour, she struggled to her feet and crept around the apartment taking stock of what was missing. His thoroughness struck her as cruel: Why had he bothered to pack the pepper grinder, the dishcloth, the spider plant, the milk he'd bought the day before? What he left behind was even worse: a photograph of her he'd had blown up, an old valentine, the sweater she'd given him.

He called late that night, his voice so flat he sounded lobotomized. "I'm really, really sorry, Barb, but I had to. I was scared of how deeply entangled we were becoming."

"What's wrong with you?" she said, crying. "You're such an asshole."

"I am not. I'm just trying to do my best. I wanted to leave now, before I hurt you any worse, because—you know—I still had doubts. I didn't want to get any closer unless I knew I could be with you for the rest of my life."

In her anger, she became fiercely logical. "But people always have doubts. That's the human condition. You never know whether you can be with someone for your entire life until it's over."

"Look, I'm sorry, but I'm sure this is the best thing for both of us," he said. She hung up on him. The phone rang again, but she didn't pick it up. Instead, she crawled into bed and curled around the one pillow he'd left. She stayed up the whole night, sometimes trembling and chattering her teeth and sometimes lying stiff with her mind racing. She had the feeling of the world shifting around her to become a place she didn't recognize, or settling with a bump like an elevator when it arrives on a floor.

* * * *

Just yesterday, she'd had the next forty years planned out for her. She and her boyfriend would stay with his family in Michigan during spring break; they'd have a clutch put in their car; they'd maybe get married and maybe retire together and live on a house-boat. Actually, these had all been his plans. He thought in great swatches of time. "I don't know if I can be with you forever," he'd say once in a while. When he got in those moods, she could sense—even when she wasn't touching him—how his muscles pulled into themselves, how he was a turtle with no shell to withdraw into.

"There isn't any such thing as forever," she'd say, trying to sound calm. She didn't need the promise of marriage or a houseboat to know she belonged with him. Instead, her certainty came in flashes, during odd and humble moments of happiness: when they lay in bed reading poems to each other in ridiculous *Masterpiece Theater* voices; or when they wandered through the cereal aisle, arguing over which artificial-colored brand they would buy and binge on as they drove home; or the night she couldn't find her shoe, and as they searched through the apartment, they had composed a song about a sneaker that lands in a beaker and becomes part of an experiment to make humanity meeker.

When the windows in Barb's bedroom turned pale with sickly morning light, she sat up, hugging the pillow between her stomach and knees. She had never thought about her future much, but now she would have to, now that he'd taken it with him like the rug, the pepper grinder, the shelves. Her life gaped before her, a new calendar with an endless line of white squares to fill in.

What would she do with herself? it occurred to her that soon—in a few months, perhaps—she'd start dating again. This would involve going to movies she wouldn't ordinarily see and having intense discussions in coffee houses with bearded men. Her stomach clenched in dread. Last time she was single she'd been twenty-seven; now she was thirty. It seemed to her the rules might have changed. While she was on sabbatical, men and women might have developed some new way of flirting that she would not understand.

But worse than the dating was the falling in love. It revolted her to think of adoring some guy and then tumbling into bed with him and the sickly sweet happiness and the fights early on and meeting his mother and moving in together and then ending up here again, hunched in sheets that still smelled of him. it seemed to her that this whole stream of events would happen over and over throughout her life, like some fever dream where you're running down a tilted hall, running and running but you never get to the end.

When the clock on the night table said 7:00, she pulled a blanket around herself and padded into the kitchen, brewed some coffee, and poured a bowl of cereal. She found she couldn't eat, but the coffee—bitter, black, and silty—went down like medicine. A few minutes later, when the caffeine hit, she threw off the blanket and dressed in cowboy boots, a short skirt, lipstick, eyeliner—the whole girlie bit. Then, to kill time before work, she took a long walk through the back streets of her neighborhood.

Her boots made crisp little clicks on the sidewalk—a sound she'd always associated with sexy and dangerous women. Yes, yes, yes, she had it all figured out. She would flirt the way she used to in the old days, go wild, and eventually settle down with someone who was good for her.

And why shouldn't she be able to find someone good this time? After all, she knew a lot of happy couples. Her friends Jim and Trish had just had a baby. Her co-worker Janet lived with this great girlfriend who made tempeh-nut loaves and could tune an engine. David and Jonathan just moved up to Vermont together. Robert and Theodore. Alice and Mimi. Christopher and Anthony….

Suddenly the truth hit her like a kick in the head. She stopped short in the middle of the sidewalk and stood there, running one finger over her lip, while the sky glowed with the color of morning glories behind the dull charcoal of the roofs. How could she have never noticed it before? It was the gay people who stayed together.

In her circle of friends, she could only name one straight couple that had lasted. Mostly, the heterosexuals lived alone, read the personals, and gulped down Prozac. Even when they did manage to fall in love, the straight people usually ended up in couples therapy—as if men and women needed professional help just to sleep together on a long-term basis. As if heterosexual desire was a bright and doomed comet that plummeted through the sky—scattering behind it a plume of therapy bills, condom wrappers, and prescriptions for pills—before it inevitably burned out.

But the gay people—they never seemed to need couples therapy. They shared beautiful apartments crammed with hand-made pottery and mementos of their life together. They drove to Provincetown for the weekend in their cars with pink-triangle bumper stickers. They held potlucks to celebrate their anniversaries, the table overflowing with candles, glazed cranberries, and red wine. They understood each other as only people of the same gender can, like sisters, like brothers, like equal partners.

Barb no longer wanted to be a part of it, the whole heterosexual thing. And suddenly she knew exactly what she had to do.

She brought up her idea with Janet a few days later when they were alone in the office together—the volunteers had all crapped out on them, so they were stuffing flyers about solid waste into preprinted envelopes.

"I've made up my mind, and I want to be a lesbian," Barb said.

"Oh jeez," Janet shook her head. She was a delicate woman with spidery hands and black hair pulled into a ponytail. "You guys just broke up. You might get back together. Anything could happen."

"We're not going to get back together. I can tell. Besides, I don't want to be with him. I don't trust him." Barb heard her voice shake as she said this.

She'd been feeling all right when she was at work, with the soothing presence of Janet nearby; and the phones ringing; and the solid-waste problem to worry about, all those landfills heaping high into the air and leaking poisons into the water supply. But when she went home—to the bare walls and the single pillow—she felt like a ghost. "The idea of not being a straight woman anymore is the only thing that makes me happy," she said.

"All right now, chill," Janet said, putting down a stack of envelopes and swiveling in her chair so she faced Barb. "Give yourself some time before you think about getting involved with anybody at all, of any gender, okay? Because you're just fixating on this as a way to escape what's really going on."

Barb laughed a little, "Okay, so I'm fixating. But, jeez, you're letting me down. I mean, what kind of lesbian are you? You're supposed to be recruiting me. Isn't that what Jesse Helms says you guys do? Well, I'm walking into the recruiting office, and I'm signing up."

"Okay, fine, you're walking into the recruiting office. And I'm determining that you're of unsound mind," Janet said. "You probably can't pass the physical, either."

"Yes, I can," Barb said, suddenly serious.

"No, I mean it. Are you really attracted to women?"

"I think so. It's hard to tell."

"What do you mean it's hard to tell?" Janet's voice was getting high, annoyed. "Sexual attraction is a very obvious thing. Do you get crushes on women? Do you fantasize about them?"

"Well, yeah, I do get crushes on women," Barb said hesitantly. "But I don't know if that's just friendship. Like once, I met this woman who immediately became my new best friend, and I used to ride my bike past her house just to see if her light was on. I wanted to be with her all the time."

"So," Janet said, squinting her eyes, "but was it sexual?"

"I don't know. Maybe there are friendship crushes, too. It did feel different from a crush on a guy, but that could be because I'm programmed to think of guys as potential boyfriends. It would be easier to tell if there were another gender, you know, a third sex that I wasn't attracted to at all. Then I'd have something to compare women to."

For days after that, Barb kept thinking about the third sex. She imagined them as squat and hairy, with thin lips and sacklike breasts dangling from their chests. She would find them ugly, though many of them would be her dear friends. She pictured herself having dinner with one of these people, its simian face relaxing into a kind expression. "Oh, Barb," it would say to her, "I care about you so much, and I'll always be there for you." She tried to imagine what else it would say, but she couldn't quite—in her mind, the third-sex person kept turning into a dumpy, awkward guy who had a crush on her.

The truth was, she couldn't imagine any close friendship that wasn't more or less a romance—there would always be unequal affections, jealousies, infatuations, even an attachment to each other's bodies. Why would things be any different with a third sex? For instance, what if Barb called the third-sex person one evening and it picked up and said, "Oh sorry, Barb, I'm on the other line. But listen, I'll get back to you as soon as I have some time"? Certainly, Barb would feel jilted.

When the third sex call-waited her, or excluded her from its dinner parties, or didn't laugh at her jokes, then she would wish for a fourth sex. And when the fourth sex failed her, she would wish for a fifth sex and a sixth—any sex, any sex at all that she could love without getting hurt.

When she was seven, her best friend, Tammy, said, "I found out how our parents sit when they're trying to make a baby. You want to see?"

She clambered over to Barb. "Here, get up. Put your legs like this." She pushed Barb's body into position, so that Barb squatted with her knees bent double and her hands behind her for support.

"Oow," Barb said, "This hurts."

Barb kept thinking about the third sex. She imagined them as squat and hairy, with thin lips and sacklike breasts.

"You get used to it. I've been practicing." Tammy lowered herself in front of Barb, so close that their legs jammed together and their stomachs almost touched. For a moment, they squatted together like two frogs.

"This is how they do it," Tammy said, rocking back and forth.

"Hey, quit it. You're pushing too hard," Barb protested, and then lost her balance and tumbled backward. She got up, brushing grass off her shorts. "Jeez. I can't believe my parents did that. That's so gross. I'll never do that."

"I know. Me either." Tammy had said, still squatting.

"Do you promise?"

"Yes."

"Really? For your whole life? Even if you really want a baby?"

"Yes," Tammy said, getting up solemnly. "I hate babies. And I'm not going to get married because I hate boys, too. My brothers are so gross. Jeff drinks milk and it comes out his nose."

Tammy had smooth skin that turned brown in the sun. She could do a handstand in or out of the water. She climbed high in trees, her P.F. Flyers slipping and kicking and scuffing the bark. In Tammy's backyard, they built a fort out of a tarp, an old doghouse, and some sticks. They would crawl in there, loving the murky light, the way sounds outside became muffled and their own voices turned as hollow as echoes. In the back of the doghouse, they kept *Archie* comics, old issues of *Arizona Highways*, candles, and a jar of Pillsbury Redi-Made icing. They ate spoonfuls of the icing only on special occasions, and it would have been the highest betrayal for one of them to open the jar when the other was not around.

Inside the fort, they spoke of solemn things. For instance, divorce. Barb lived with her mother; her father had had his own apartment ever since she could remember. He came for dinners on Sunday. The whole time he was there, Barb would catch her parents giving each other dirty looks—those looks hurt like nails sticking into her skin.

"The way you can tell if a kid's parents are divorced? If you go over to his house, or her house, or whatever? You know how you can tell?" Barb had explained one day. "The kid will have a Mexican puppet. The parents get

divorced in Mexico, and they bring you back a present from there. I guess the only good toys in Mexico are puppets."

"But how can you tell if your parents are going to be divorced?" Tammy had asked. She sat under the place where the tarp bulged out, which made her voice sound as hollow as a ghost's.

"I don't know."

"Barb?" Tammy said in that strange voice, "What do I do if it happens?"

"We can live in our fort. Even if all our parents move away, we'll stay here. We should start saving food. And we'll need a flashlight," Barb said.

"But what about the new people who move into my house? They won't let us stay here, will they?"

"No, it'll be okay. We'll just explain that we need to live here. Don't worry, they won't kick us out. Maybe they'll have a dog we can play with." Sometimes Barb actually hoped all their parents would move away so that she and Tammy could camp in the fort every night, eating frosting and studying the pictures in *Arizona Highways* by candlelight. They liked to touch the closeups of the cacti, pretending that the needles were pricking their fingers. "Ouch," "ouch," "ouch, that smarts," they would say, patting the smooth paper.

One morning—this was a month and a half after Barb's boyfriend had moved out—she walked into the office and Janet called out, "Is that the lesbian?"

Barb wedged into Janet's gray-walled cubicle. "Who me?"

Janet was leaning over in her chair to unlace her boots. "Yeah you."

"I thought you refused to encourage me in this whole lesbian thing."

"Well, I wasn't going to, but I'm afraid circumstances are now beyond my control. There's a girl who's hot for you."

"No way. Really?" Barb drumrolled her hands gleefully on the desk. "Yes. Yes. Yes. Who is it? Is it somebody I met at your party?" Janet had given a brunch that weekend—a tumult of straight couples, gay couples, babies, dogs, pasta salads, tofu spreads.

"Yeah," Janet said, taking a tiny sip of her coffee and then waving her hand in front of her mouth, as if to cool it off. "Remember that woman you talked to? A few inches shorter than you, dark skin, crew out, real cute."

"Huh?" Barb said. "Oh yeah, I guess I remember. But I didn't really talk to her. I think I asked her where to find the cups. Oh, and then we talked about how we both like seltzer water."

"Well," Janet sighed, "that must have been some conversation, because she called me afterward and wanted the low-down. God knows I warned her about you, but she wouldn't listen. Listen, Rita's really nice, but unfortunately she always falls for hopeless cases such as yourself. If you go out with her, you've got to promise you'll be careful. I don't want you leading her on and then deciding you're really straight. Do you understand?" she said sternly.

"All I did was talk to her about seltzer water. So sue me. I'll probably never even see her again."

Janet was silent a moment. Then she said, "Rita's going to call you. I gave her your number. I hope that's all right."

Barb felt a pang in her stomach. "Sure, yeah, that's fine. I just didn't expect it to happen so fast. I had all these plans for the things I was going to do before I actually went out with a woman."

"Like, what?"

"I thought I'd read *Rubyfruit Jungle* first. Maybe join an all-women's softball team. I still haven't gone through that whole pre-paratory phase, you know, like you went through in high school."

"Well if you're not ready yet, just say the word. I'll tell Rita." Janet turned away to log in to her computer.

"No, no, it's okay. I'm ready. Frankly, it would be a big relief to just sleep with a woman, so I could consider myself a les-bian. I hate this in-between thing. Right now, I feel like I'm a nothing—I'm not straight anymore, but I'm not gay either. It sucks."

Barb was referring to how she felt when-ever she walked through the sliding doors and into the vitamin-scented air of the food co-op. She'd always heard that place was a big pickup spot, but when she lived with her boyfriend she hadn't paid much attention to the glances people shot at one another over the kale, the way the cashiers sometimes flirted with her.

Nowadays, though, the food co-op seemed to steam with sexuality. When men lingered near her in the aisle, she admired their sinewy hands and the soft stretch of their chests; when they looked over at her, she met their eyes. She was equally moved by the beauty of women, their ripe lips and the swell of their butts.

She even found herself attracted to the bearded dyke who worked in the produce department. Just a few months ago, Barb had found this particular woman frightening: she had a little goatee like Shaggy from *Scooby Doo*, a pierced nose, and blond hair that hung in a heavy braid. Back when Barb lived with her boyfriend, she'd dismissed the woman as a nutcase. That way she never had to think about the beard and all it implied.

But now Barb did think about the beard—a lot. While she was waiting for a bus or washing dishes, she would meditate on the beard, trying to remember exactly how the hair sprouted from the woman's pointed chin, how it was thick at the sides but became wispy under her lips, like a goat's whiskers.

The beard raised all kinds of questions. For instance, did it grow naturally or did the woman have to rub some kind of potion on her chin? If the beard grew naturally, then how many other women would also have furry faces if they didn't bleach and tweeze away the evidence? And if the world was full of bearded women, then what did that mean about our bodies? Did people resort to electrolysis, hair transplants, tummy tucks, breast implants, and perfumes not so much to make themselves beautiful as to hide the shameful truth—the truth of men's breasts and women's beards and the sagging genderlessness of old age? At heart, are all our bodies cross-dressers?

If she would only pluck and bleach, the bearded woman in the produce department might have resembled a young Judy Collins—she had gorgeous, wide-set eyes and golden skin. But she didn't pluck. She didn't bleach. She had chosen to turn herself into

something impossible to define, not exactly a man or a woman, not exactly a lesbian either.

"Are you attracted to women with beards?" Barb asked Janet once.

"Oh, please. I don't know too many girls who want to suck a hairy face. Frankly, I think dykes grow beards because they don't want to be sexual at all. They want to scare people off."

But when Barb caught a glimpse of that woman hauling boxes—the muscles working in her lean arms—she knew the woman didn't want to scare anyone off. In fact, the woman managed to be sexy in the most original manner Barb had ever witnessed— her sexiness had nothing to do with gender but simply came from her own presence, the comfortable swing of her arms and sheen of sweat on her forehead. She was sexy in the way of a cat, an orchid, a clump of hair, a cut-open tomato.

Two days later, Rita left a message on Barb's machine. Her voice sounded breathy, scared. Barb imagined how Rita must have sat in front of the telephone, holding the scrap of paper with Barb's number on it; how Rita must have dialed in a daring rush, with her heart booming in her ears. All of a sudden, Barb felt very close to this woman. She pictured Rita curled around her in bed, holding her from behind the way her boyfriend used to do. But when she dialed Rita's number and a stranger's voice said, "Hello?" the whole holding-each-other-in-bed scenario seemed ridiculous.

"Hi, Rita? I just got your message. This is Barb."

The person at the other end of the line cleared her throat. "Hi, Barb. I hope you don't mind that I called."

"No, I'm glad—"

"It's just that I thought you were interesting and, um, I was hoping you'd want to maybe hang out and talk sometime," Rita gushed.

"Oh, okay, sure. How about this weekend?"

"We could invite Janet, too, if you want."

"No, that's all right," Barb said. "I love Janet, but we already spend forty hours a week together. By the way, how do you know her?"

"We were in an African drumming class together a long time ago. Oh yeah, and her girlfriend was a housemate of mine." Rita laughed nervously. "I guess I know her a bunch of different ways."

"African drumming, huh?"

"I'm in this band. We play Caribbean-influenced dance music."

"Wow. Huh. Interesting." Barb could feel her face splitting in a false smile.

"Yeah, it's fun."

The silence between them lasted a second too long.

"Well," Barb said, "where do you want to meet?"

After she hung up, she began scrubbing the kitchen. The call had acted on her like a cup of coffee drunk too late in the day—it made her nervous, scattered, and obsessed with getting the grease off her stove.

She'd done all the dishes and was about to wipe the table when she suddenly stopped dead in front of the refrigerator, transfixed by the photo of Tammy. She had just recently found that picture, and without knowing why, had taken it to the kitchen and hung it next to the pictures of her current friends.

Now she slid the magnets off the curling picture and held it close to her face. There was Tammy in a 1970s zip-up shirt pretending to strangle a Barbie doll. Examining the picture, Barb could make out the wallpaper in her own childhood bedroom—she'd forgotten all about that pattern of balloony psychedelic flowers until just now.

She used to stare at those flowers in the half-darkness as she fell asleep, watching how they turned into the faces of gossipy old women; at the same time, she would listen to her mother downstairs, the way the click-click-click of those heels tapped out a message: "I'm taking care of everything down here. We got it all under control."

Suddenly Barb was overcome by a sickening loneliness. She wanted, more than anything, to be back in her old bedroom. Or better yet, to return to the fort, to be pressed up against Tammy as they plunged plastic spoons into the can of frosting and laughed so hard that they snorted snot out of their noses.

When they both were ten, Tammy's parents got divorced and Tammy herself suddenly turned into a stranger: she got herself a Campus Queen lunchbox and began running around with the popular girls, administering cootie shots to the boys. But before that—back when Barb and Tammy were still best friends and spent summer evenings in the fort listening to the cicadas screech—they had made a pact.

"When we grow up, we'll have our own house," Tammy had said. "With a pool."

"I want one of those water slides, like they have at King's Dominion."

"But we'll have our own house," Tammy had said firmly. "Okay?"

"Yeah." Barb pictured a house made of tarp and sticks, a giant version of their fort.

"That means that when you grow up, you have to find me, okay? Because I don't know where I'll be." Tammy let out a sigh. "We're probably going to move, you know."

"Okay," Barb said.

To make it official they had chanted together, "Cross my heart, hope to die, stick a needle in my eye."

"And if we don't find each other and live in our house together," Barb said, "we really have to stick needles in our eyes, okay?"

Once, she had been willing to stick a needle in her eye—anything, anything to stay in that fort with Tammy. So how had she come to this? How had she become a woman who paced around her apartment alone and met strangers in cafés? After all, she was the girl who loved to share musty issues of *Arizona Highways*, plastic spoons, slightly used Band-Aids, hair clips. She was the girl who loved to share his car; who slept on his sheets with their maplike stains; who woke up with him pressed against her back, as if he were trying to see over her shoulder or push himself further into her life.

"Well, it's not like I can't sing. I choose not to," Rita was saying. Then she started giggling and rubbed her face with one hand. "I don't know why I'm telling you this. I feel like I'm babbling."

"You're not babbling," Barb said. "You're just enthusiastic."

"I guess I am enthusiastic, even though I get scared when we perform. I really like that feeling of being in synch with other people, knowing what they're going to do before they even do it."

Rita's close-shaved black hair turned blue and shadowy at the nape of her neck. She wore a cinnamon-colored sweater so big on her that the sleeves covered the tips of her fingers. She had a habit of gesturing emphatically with these sleeve-covered hands that Barb found endearing.

"So when can I see you guys play?" Barb said.

"Oh no way, no way," Rita flopped one of her sweater-hands at Barb. "We're going to be at El Diablo's on Saturday but you're not allowed to come."

Barb found herself laughing. "You can't stop me, you know. It's a free country."

"No, I'm serious. If you're there, I'll get nervous and flub up."

"You're not really nervous; that's just something you're pretending so I won't notice how smooth an operator you are," Barb said, arching an eyebrow. She was surprised at her own flirtatiousness.

Though all she was doing, really, was following Rita's lead. Rita was the one who had initiated the flirting when, two hours ago, she had swept into the cafe and dumped her bag beside Barb's table. "I had to be late," she blurted out, settling opposite Barb in the booth, "because it would have been too nerve-racking if I were the one waiting for you. I would have been worried that you were going to blow me off."

And so they had talked and talked in a too-much-coffee frenzy, the way people do when they're interested in each other. For yes, even though the phone call had been awkward, Barb had become more and more attracted to Rita as they talked in the café—not Rita's body so much as the whole bubbling mess of her. It was the flirting that made Barb feel attracted, the flit of their eyes, the intensity of their conversation, the hints they dropped about seeing each other again. Flirting was like a trial-size bottle of sex, Barb realized; you could sample what it was like to be intimate with the other person, but you didn't have to strip naked. Flirting was like a dance, a series of bows and feints where you touched hands but never came too close.

And in this dance, this dance here at the table with Rita, Barb was the man. She wore a tux and stepped in squares while Rita, in a red dress, flew around her. Sometimes even when she'd been with men, Barb had felt like she was the man—the powerful one, the one at the center of the other person's fluttery dance. But she had never felt so much the man as now.

"Oh God," Rita said. "Does this muffin taste like vomit or what? Try some and tell me if I'm crazy." She slid her plate toward Barb, and they both leaned in close to it, as if examining something of extreme importance.

Barb picked off a few crumbs and put them in her mouth. "Too much lemon peel," she said authoritatively.

"You think?" Rita said, and then her eyes settled on her watch. "Oh shit. I've got to

go pick up my car at the shop before they close." She said this last in a businesslike voice and then turned soft again. "Look, I really do have to go. I'm not lying. I mean, I hope we can see each other again."

"Sure," Barb said.

Rita rubbed her cheek with one sweater-covered hand. "But if you don't want to, I understand," she added. She had this waiting-to-be-slapped expression on her face, as if she expected Barb to say something cruel; as if she was preparing herself to love someone who couldn't love her back; as if already she could imagine the calls Barb would fail to return, the anniversary she would forget, the things Barb would leave in her apartment when they broke up.

Seeing Rita like that, Barb had an urge to go to the other side of the booth and slide in beside her. She wanted to hug Rita, to soothe her with friendly words. What would she say? "You don't have to try so hard." Or maybe, "Don't expect so much." Or maybe, "Let's quit now before things get out of hand."

But Barb couldn't leave her side of the booth. She was stuck there, across the table from Rita. The two of them were already locked in their dance. They were whirling around each other, twirling, bowing, dipping. And it was everything she remembered—the gleaming top hat, the tails, the swirling satin dress, the high heels, the cummerbund, the stiff kid gloves.

Dating Tips and Treatises

Seventies Survivors

I have this theory: Those who grew up during or after the 1970s never learned how to date. Sure, we know how to meet someone at a party and fall into bed with them. Sure, we know how to dull the ache of a breakup by reaching for the next convenient person. But we're hopeless when it comes to the old-fashioned art of socializing with several prospective partners at once—without bedding any of them. We in the maturing hipster community are especially guilty of this. Let's face it, many of us think we're too cool to go through the hopelessly mainstream ritual of meeting people for coffee and chatting about movies. We have imagined a utopia where no one has to date anymore; we fantasize that our true love will suddenly materialize at the next yard sale or pro-choice demonstration. Maturing hipsters, I say to you, it's time to face the cold, hard truth. You're probably not going to find love unless you put in a lot of legwork first. Sure, dating's uncool. Sure, calling someone up to ask them to go to the movies with you doesn't exactly make you feel like a cultural outlaw. Want to feel like a real cultural outlaw? How about spending the rest of your life holed up in your tiny apartment with nothing but your rare Jackie Chan posters and your collection of Re/Search books to keep you company?

E-Mail

One friend of mine went on an E-mail bender, corresponding with no less than five virtual boyfriends at any one time. She even slept with one of the guys she met online, but—since he turned out to be a harmless yet annoying psycho—she never did find her Romeo in cyberspace. In fact, nobody I know has ever had a virtual flirtation that turned into a real relationship. Still, cyber-whatever has its uses. It's pretty darn convenient if you're too strung out for real-life romance or if there's…some other reason you can't go on dates. My friend who had all the E-mail boyfriends? She was still sharing an apartment with her sort-of ex-boyfriend. (She couldn't afford to live alone, nor did she have the energy to throw him out.) This hellish situation made it impossible for her to date, so she retreated to her PC, where she could be a secret swinger.

I had my own brief cyber-fling. I'd just been through a bad breakup and was still hurting, though I was going out with various guys. Actually, the dates only depressed me more—with every awkward moment sitting across from a stranger in a café, I became more and more convinced that I'd never be in a relationship again. And then I checked my E-mail one morning and found a message from some guy I'd met at a party who had a desperate crush on me. (I'd talked to a lot of people that night and couldn't remember which one he was.) So began our correspondence. He turned out to be funny, sweet, and—when I finally agreed to meet him—a walking heap of unrealistic expectations and raw nerves. But thanks partly to him, my own raw nerves started to heal. Our E-mail flirtation felt safe and, oddly, like a practice session or a set of exercises.

Cyber-dating is great. It's the StairMaster of love—you use it to keep in shape, not to climb to where you want to be.

Dating Tips and Treatises

Unsafe at Any Speed

Once, a friend of mine insisted that I read a certain dating self-help book. She said it had changed her life. I found the book revolting and symbolic of all that's wrong with America today—yet its ideas seeped into my psyche.

Briefly, the book is by a woman who decided to get married within one year and succeeded. She details her method: She placed a personal ad and screened her "applicants"; then she narrowed the field down to two suitors and drew up sophisticated lists and charts to decide between them. The book warns that you must not let some nonmarriageable guy sweep you off your feet; instead, you should figure out exactly what you want and then go out and find the guy who fills the bill. The self-help writer insisted that love doesn't have to be a scary plunge down a rollercoaster; it could be sensible and sane, kind of like a business merger.

I have to admit, this idea appealed to me. And when I met a guy who called me like clockwork and had worked at the same saving-the-environment job for ten years, a guy who was absolutely reliable and never said anything that surprised me, I decided, "This is what I need." After years of trusting my heart to flaky boyfriends, I'd finally put my heart somewhere safe.

But meanwhile, I kept dating other people before I made any decision (which, to its credit, the self-help book recommended). There was this other guy who kept calling me, and I decided to go out to dinner with him. On our first date Guy B told me he was about to move to Vietnam and so he couldn't really be in a relationship; when he saw my house, he commented that my porch would make the perfect sniper's nest; he also confessed he'd once had an infection on his head that had gotten so bad it turned into a green worm of puss that fell off one day in the shower with a splat. After we parted that night, I was laughing to myself about how incredibly wrong this Mr. Wrong was. Yeah, and just guess who I fell in love with. And guess who I'm living with a year and a half later.

The Tao of Dating

"Desire and wanting cause discontent, whilst he who knows sufficiency more easily has what he requires." So says ancient philosopher Lao-tzu. He's talking, of course, about sex appeal. Happiness is sexy. Neediness isn't.

Before the sexual revolution, women were supposed to play hard to get in order to hide their neediness. Now certain reactionary forces are urging us to adopt this strategy again. As I write, a book called *The Rules* sits atop the bestseller list; the authors urge you to act bitchy, turn down dates, make him pay for your dinner; they say you should never ask him out first, nor should you speak until you're spoken to. I prefer the Taoist solution. If you're already content with your life, then you honestly don't give a shit whether or not your date likes you—and your indifference makes you seem incredibly desirable to him or her. Enlightenment comes to those who pass through the gateless gate. Sex appeal comes to those who have learned to go on the dateless date.

Dating Tips and Treatises

Pretend to go to the bathroom and never come back if:

- You sense that your date has been through a twelve-step program and has no sense of humor about it. Phrases to watch out for: *my last relationship was toxic*; *I grew up in a shaming household; I need a partner who can mirror me.*
- He brings you flowers on the second or third date. I know that sounds awfully harsh, but think about it: What do flowers really mean? Probably that he's completely tuned out your bizarre sense of style or your obsession with bats or your talent for playing Hungarian fiddle music or whatever. Flowers mean that he's just taking shots in the dark in hopes that he may get laid. Of course, exceptions can be made for any guy who gives dead flowers or plastic mistletoe.
- You realize that she's got a checklist in her head and she's checking off items as she talks to you. *High-paying job? No. Able to pick the best wine off the list? No. Attention to personal hygiene? No.*

These philosophies of dating that I just shared with you helped me find this man. And once he was mine, I forced this hairstyle on him. Okay, okay, I know. I'm being as bad as the self-help author who "proved" her dating method worked because she managed to bag a man within one year. Look, in my saner moments, I'm sure that the point of dating is not to find true love, not exactly. The point of dating is that we—motivated by our loneliness or our lust or our hope that somewhere waits a person who will really understand the whirling thoughts locked inside our skulls—get off our butts and take some life-changing, hair-raising risks.

PERSONAL CARE

Esso

Soy milk

I'd rather be trash picking

As far as I know, no one had a lifestyle before the 1970s; oh sure, your average Joe might have had hobbies and habits, but he probably didn't think too much about the minutiae of his existence—what he ate or what he wore or how he expressed his feelings. Then hippie culture hit the mainstream, the word lifestyle entered popular parlance, and your average Joe was confronted with a lot of weird shit: primal-scream therapy, androgyny, open marriages, space food. Suddenly he needed to be able to know whether he was into vegetarian cooking or French cuisine, surfing or ceramics, EST or Christ.

More than twenty years later, we take this whole lifestyle thing for granted. Of course everyone has their own special dietary needs; of course we all have our own exercise regimens; of course we heal ourselves with a mixture of Eastern and Western medicines. According to a recent study, one-third of America practices some sort of New Age treatment or spiritual ritual. In most malls these days, you can find a boutique that sells crystals, Buddhas, and "Indian" dream catchers. New Age and "alternative," ideas have become so watered down that many of them actually strike us as conservative now—from the touchy-feely style of modern political speeches to the practice of taking megadoses of vitamins.

Enough of lifestyles. It's time for "lifesystems." That's the word I just invented to describe how some of my friends cope. They develop their own eccentric outlook on politics or religion, throw in a bunch of obsessive behaviors, and then tie the whole thing together with an overarching philosophy. For instance, my friend Chris is a urine-drinking, cross-dressing, Luddite antipopulationist with his own Web site. While none of his habits or ideas necessarily belong together, he's managed to mesh them into his own personal religion/ health regimen. It works for him.

A lifesystem: You come up with a moral position on everything from eating eggs to flushing the toilet and then you try your darndest to stick to it. It's like a belief system, only more detail-oriented.

Since When Were Hipsters in Shape?

THE FIRST TIME I WORE LYCRA WAS IN 1990. MY FRIEND LOANED ME SHORTS SO I COULD GO RUNNING WITH HER.

YOU DON'T UNDERSTAND. I CAN'T DO THIS. I'VE PLEDGED NEVER TO WEAR LYCRA.

OH COME ON, PAGAN. ARE YOU THAT AFRAID OF BEING UNCOOL?

THE LYCRA WORKED A STRANGE MAGIC, EVENING OUT THE BULGES, SO MY LEGS LOOKED JOCK-LIKE. A DANGEROUS IDEA ENTERED MY HEAD: MAYBE I COULD BE ATHLETIC!

I'D ALWAYS EXERCISED -- IN FACT, I DID A THOUSAND-MILE BIKE TRIP IN HIGH SCHOOL-- BUT CONSIDERED MYSELF HOPELESS AT ATHLETICS. SO DID MOST OTHER PEOPLE I KNEW.

ME TOO

IN JUNIOR HIGH, I ALWAYS GOT PICKED LAST FOR EVERY TEAM. I WAS SO UNCOORDINATED.

SOMETIMES IT SEEMED LIKE EVERY ALTERNATIVE LIFESTYLE WAS INVENTED BY PEOPLE WHO'D BEEN TRAUMATIZED BY HIGH SCHOOL GYM CLASS.

GOTH ROCKERS

FEMINISTS WITH FOOD ISSUES

DRUG USERS

STRESSED-OUT ACTIVISTS

SEMIOTICIANS

AND THEN THE CULTURAL MOOD CHANGED. BEING OBSESSED WITH YOUR BODY NO LONGER SEEMED HOPELESSLY MAINSTREAM. GEEKS LIKE ME STARTED WEARING LYCRA. AND POST-MODERN POP INTELLECTUALS LIKE KATHY ACKER STARTED BODY BUILDING.

My main sexual relationship is with my motorcycle...
I've been going to this rolfer...
I asked [Robert Bly] if he wanted to see my piercings. He wouldn't do it...
I don't have a text outside my body that I want to impose on my body in some kind of fascistic way.*

*all quotes real

BY THE WAY, HAVER YOU NOTICED THAT KATHY ACKER LOOKS JUST LIKE A CERTAIN OTHER CELEB?

STOP THE INSANITY!

WELL, I ADMIT IT: I, TOO, YIELDED TO THE "MADONNAFICATION" OF ALTERNATIVE CULTURE—THE NEW AESTHETIC THAT SAID BODIES ARE TO BE SCULPTED INSTEAD OF IGNORED. I JOINED A GYM IN '92. ONCE, MY FRIENDS WOULD HAVE TAUNTED ME. NOW THEY WANTED TO MEET ME THERE.

AT FIRST I WAS SHOCKED AT WHAT WAS CONSIDERED NORMAL IN MY ALL-WOMEN'S GYM.

19-YEAR-OLD HEAD CASES.

MIRRORS EVERYWHERE

ME? THIN? MY THIGHS ARE SACKS OF BLUBBER MY GOAL THIS SUMMER IS TO LOSE AN INCH OFF EACH ONE.

ANOREXICS KILLING THEMSELVES RIGHT OUT IN PUBLIC

BUTT FLOSS

I TRIED TO GET IN SHAPE WITHOUT GETTING BRAINWASHED.

I'LL DO THE AEROBICS BUT I REFUSE TO CLAP OR YELL "WOO WOO."

BUT WITHIN A YEAR OR SO....

HMM... IT'S 5 O'CLOCK. IF I HURRY, I'LL JUST MAKE THE STEP 'N' FUNK CLASS.

WORKING OUT HAS MADE MY LIFE RICHER. AFTER A HARD DAY OF BEING AN ANGST-RIDDEN ARTIST, NOTHING RESTORES ME TO SANITY LIKE GOING TO THE GYM. AND I'M FINALLY BECOMING COORDINATED, SO I CAN DO ALL SORTS OF THINGS THAT USED TO SEEM IMPOSSIBLE.

YOUR SERVE IS GETTING GOOD!

WHO AM I? HAVE I BECOME ONE OF THOSE PERKY NORMAL PEOPLE I USED TO DESPISE?

MY BOYFRIEND, EX-JOCK

STILL, I THINK WE WERE RIGHT TO BE SUSPICIOUS. WHAT IS "GETTING IN SHAPE" BESIDES WHITTLING OUR BODIES INTO SAMENESS?

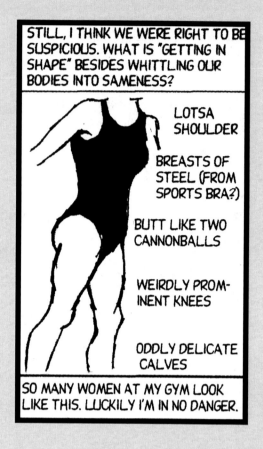

LOTSA SHOULDER

BREASTS OF STEEL (FROM SPORTS BRA?)

BUTT LIKE TWO CANNONBALLS

WEIRDLY PROM-INENT KNEES

ODDLY DELICATE CALVES

SO MANY WOMEN AT MY GYM LOOK LIKE THIS. LUCKILY I'M IN NO DANGER.

THINK ABOUT IT: THE PEOPLE WITH THE MOST LIBER-ATED MINDS HAVE USUALLY HAD "BAD" BODIES.

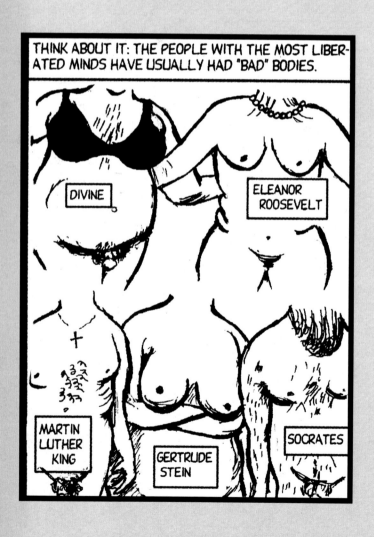

DIVINE

ELEANOR ROOSEVELT

MARTIN LUTHER KING

GERTRUDE STEIN

SOCRATES

MOST PEOPLE WHO'VE FOUGHT FOR SOCIAL JUSTICE HAVEN'T HAD TIME TO TONE THEIR ABS. MOREOVER, I THINK TOO MUCH EXERCISE CALMS YOU, MAKES IT EASIER TO ACCEPT THE STATUS QUO.

REMEMBER WHEN DEVO URGED US ALL TO BECOME "BEAUTIFUL MUTANTS"? REMEMBER THE FAT, HAIRY HIPPIES OF HOGG FARM? REMEMBER WALT WHIT-MAN LUSTING AFTER ANYTHING THAT MOVED? WHAT THE HELL HAS HAPPENED TO THIS COUNTRY? WHEN DID WE ALL GET SO SUPER-FICIAL AND VAIN?

STOP THE INANITY!

Call-wait (v.). Some phone users will say, "Hang on, okay? I've got another call." Then they'll click onto their other line, and leave you for many long minutes—during which you feel like an idiot because you're stuck there with the receiver pressed to your ear. You have just been call-waited. To be *call-waited* is to be snubbed in a subtle way, as in, "Angela, don't you dare *call-wait* me when we're in the middle of an argument."

Worse, of course, is to be *call-dumped*—that's when your friend comes back on the line and says, "Look, I've got to take this one. I'll get you later, okay?"

Chain-smoke. If you run through a series of intense, short-term affairs, you are *chain-smoking*. Generally used to describe a condition in which someone's love life has become an elaborate nervous habit: "Remember when James was trying to finish his dissertation? He got really depressed and started *chain-smoking* girlfriends until he met Natalie."

Friendly fire. The best thing about a corporate job is being laid off. If you're lucky, you can end up with a generous severance package, and when that runs out, unemployment benefits. All told, you may end up with a six-month all-expense-paid vacation in your apartment. Several friends of mine have held on to their jobs for months and months as their companies went down the tubes, waiting for that glorious pink slip. They were hoping for a *friendly fire*—as in, "Did you hear John just lost his job at Acme Corp? He's really happy, because it was a *friendly fire*, so now he can go to cafés and work on his screenplay for a while."

In the zone. It's standard knowledge that dating is either feast or famine. Either you haven't gotten laid in months or else you've got five people chasing you.

Why does this happen? Maybe some guy from work flirts with you and that makes you feel a tad sexy. Which leads to somebody else admitting he has a crush on you. Then you definitely feel sexy. And then the floodgates open. Suddenly you exude self—confidence, and your body probably begins spewing pheromones into the air. Guys (or gals) will hover around you like bees pollinating a flower. Sales clerks will give you presents. People in post offices with ask you what kind of stamps you're buying and then want to go out for coffee. You will receive unsolicited love letters.

At this point you are in the zone. It is time to call up your friends and gloat. "I am so in the zone," you will say. "Do you know how many dates I went on this week?" But don't be too proud, because soon enough you may be knocked out of the zone. And you can never force your way back into the zone; you have to ride into it, like a surfer catching the perfect wave.

WORDS TO LIVE BY

WORDS TO LIVE BY

Mafo. WASPS are undoubtedly the ethnic group most deserving of ridicule. Therefore, it would be nice if our language provided a potpourri of slurs specifically designed to put down white Protestants. Unfortunately, language fails us in this area. Can you think of any insults that refer to WASPS in particular? There are few with any real bite. I mean, okay, there's always "honky." But that term has started to sound awfully dated—I mean, how can you call someone a honky without feeling like you're pretending to be John Shaft?

So I'd like to propose a new term: Mafo. The word, derived from "Mayflower," has a nice, obscene ring to it. Mafo works best when you use it in plural form, as in, "Sorry I was late. Bobby Short was playing downtown and all the fuckin' Mafos were milling around in the street like a herd of sheep."

Eventually Mafo might evolve into a within-group term, the Way "nigger" has been appropriated by blacks. A WASP might use the term thusly: "Chip smashed up his Beemer in Newport yesterday after imbibing a few too many bloodies. He certainly is one bad-ass *Mafo*."

Other slurs for white people:
Ofay, Cracker, Eurotrash, Lo-fan (Cantonese), **Haole** (Hawaiian, meaning outsider).

Netwad. An E-mail pal wrote in to tell me he knew he'd become a *netwad* when he spent an hour on-line trying to figure out how to get from his house to some other part of town. It would have been much easier to run down to his car and check a map, but somehow it seemed easier to get information off the Web. A netwad is a high-tech slacker who's taken the whole slacking thing too far—even getting out of a chair has become onerous.

Shaggy. A guy who fits the Generation X-slacker stereotype so perfectly that it's embarrassing, as in, "I didn't realy hold it against him when he started wearing the striped shirts and baggy pants, but when he grew a goatee, I knew he was just another *shaggy*."

Therapized (vi.). Having been subjected to a predictable course of therapy, as in, "After he was *therapized*, he lost his cynical sense of humor and started telling everyone he was an adult child of alcoholics."

Thrift (v.). When you shop at the Salvation Army or Goodwill or AMVETS, you are thrifting. I first saw *thrift* used as a verb in a zine called *Thrift Score*, edited by Al Hoff. Al urges that you greet your fellow AMVET Heads with the salutation, "Thrift on!"

Quit in place. Most people who hate their jobs eventually hand in their resignation. A few people I know have chosen a more…creative solution. They quit mentally, turning their cubicles into their own personal centers for gossiping, letter-writing, zine publishing, Web surfing, political organizing, and long-distance teleconferencing.

Web serfing. If you're hanging out on the Web on your own time, just having fun, then you're *Web serfing*. If some company is paying you to cruise around looking for insurance or rubber-hosing links, then you're *Web serfing*. Once you're paid to be on it, the Web turns from a 2-D theme park into a tortuously slow, eye-burning hell.

Weeble. Derived from the "Weebles wobble but they don't fall down" ad of the early seventies. A person who—if stripped of his or her mantle of corporate power—would be a total loser. "My boss is such a weeble. He makes me work late all the time, and I swear it's just so he'll have someone around to watch *Star Trek* with him."

Zac. Affectionate shorthand for "Prozac."

Tuning Out

Why You Might Know More
If You Stopped Following the News

For a few years I've been telling people that I'm in a "media blackout." Before adopting this policy, I was like any other urban intellectual; I would dutifully keep up with left-wing journals and hefty newspapers, considering it my responsibility to know what was going on in the world. Nonetheless, I always felt uninformed. The news never seemed to supply what I wanted—rather than giving me a sense that I understood the world, it made me dizzy and confused. I was standing in the middle of a blizzard of information, unable to see my hand in front of my face. The facts—names, policies, events—whirled around me like millions of snowflakes. I was in danger of being buried under them. So I decided to see what life was like without the news.

I tuned out the *Times.* I tuned out the *MacNeil-Lehrer Report.* I tuned out the Brits recapping world events on NPR. I let this blizzard of information die down in hopes that, with the air clear, I would finally see what was around me.

Well, okay, this story is not exactly true. What's true is that I invented the term *media blackout*; and I did go around telling people I was in one because I liked how that sounded, so melodramatic and Stalinist. But I did cheat. I continued to plow through stacks of printed matter—the *New Yorker*, certain issues of the *Times Book Review*, scare stories about deadly microbes in *Newsweek*. And I cheated inadvertently, too. I found myself picking up a lot from friends' conversations; in the food co-op, I'd hear the news on NPR; at the gym, I'd find myself Stair-Mastering in front of a TV. The media is everywhere: on that billboard and in my computer, up there over the bar, and inside my friend's head.

So maybe I should say that I'm not in a strict media blackout—I'm just doing the best I can in an environment that's polluted with information. According to one study, the average person sees 16,000 ads a day, if you include the corporate messages and symbols slapped on almost every surface of every object on Earth now. At six years old, kids have spent more time glued to the TV set than they will spend in college classes—if they go to college. TVs are moving into airport lounges, stores, buses, classrooms, subway platforms. To truly go into a media blackout you'd have to move to a Trappist monastery or perhaps build yourself a cabin in Alaska. We live not in our bodies, not in our physical surroundings, but in a jungle of signs and symbols that scream commands at us.

So how do you continue to live in a city and still black out all the distractions? There's a lot you can't do, but at least you can pay attention to what you watch and read, and decide whether you should cut down. When I reevaluated my media diet, I realized that I had to make an extra effort to avoid the "respectable" news. It's always been easy for me to ignore crap like *Entertainment Tonight*, the O.J. trial, AM-radio news, *Hard Copy, USA Today*. I'm much more susceptible to the oat bran of the media world, those unappetizing gray newspapers that are "good for me," which are supposed to transform me into an "informed citizen" and keep me up-to-date with "what's really happening." But of course the *New York Times* and the *Washington Post* are just as corporate controlled as their less respectable brethren; they are designed not to inform but to sell ads and to keep you hooked so you buy tomorrow's newspaper.

When people criticize journalism, they never seem to mention its deepest dangers. They talk about its failings in specific terms. Was that toxic spill covered in the *New York Times*? Did it appear on page 1 or page 40? How was the story slanted? These kind of questions, as important as they are, keep us from seeing the big picture. We quibble over the lettuce and sour cream, when in fact the problem is the whole enchilada.

Think about the setup of the *New York Times*, for instance—whatever liberal message you may get from a particular article or editorial, the format caters to the needs of the corporations. Does The Man want you to get your information quickly and easily? Or does he perhaps want you to sit there

for hours in front of your TV or to plow through your newspapers, exposing yourself to as many advertisements as possible? The Man is a master at keeping you plugged in, dazzled, overstimulated. When you read a newspaper, you're forced to comb through the minutiae of personalities and political ploys, the opinions of pundits, the finger-to-the-wind conjectures about the mood of the American people. You're updated on a daily basis. You're kept abreast of the candidates' wardrobe changes, the eating habits of Chinese bureaucrats, the child-rearing woes of Marcia Clark. The newspaper grabs you by the head and shoves

you face-first into a swirling miasma of information; kept in that headlock, you will never be able to step back and get a view. And political understanding depends exactly on stepping back—it depends on the broad, the sweeping, and the historical.

I want to know who decided that I have to read a newspaper every day. How did this become a middle-class ritual? Since when did being faithful to the media make anyone a good citizen? We—and here I'm talking about intellectuals, primarily—we half-believe that we'll use all the information we guzzle down from *Nightline* and the *Times*; the irony, of course, is that we end up spending so much energy gathering information that we're never able to act on it. "Oh, just one more factoid, I just need one more before I can do something about welfare cuts!" "Well, I can't very well help Kurdish refugees until I understand how this might affect the situation in Turkey and whether relief would even do any good in the first place." Newspapers keep us in a continual state of anxiety about our own lack of information. They tell us a story—a story about power brokers and behind-the-scenes deals, a story in which we can never hope to be characters. They alienate us from our own world.

If newspapers and news shows really were effective providers of information, we wouldn't need them much. We might read or watch for only a few minutes a day—or we might even begin to seek out news on a weekly or monthly basis. Have you noticed that newspapers rarely provide you with any of the information you need in order to act in the world? They don't tell you when the demonstrations will be held, where the meetings are, which congresspeople to call and what their numbers are, how to sign the petitions, or when the bus leaves for Washington. Without such practical information, the front page might as well be the sports section—you read about a game you can never participate in. And more and more, even the respectable newspapers give us news-as-spectator-sport. O.J., Tonya Harding, the debate over political correctness, *The Bell Curve*—these political footballs get tossed around to keep the crowd entertained. We are the passive audience, not the players.

I see those bumper stickers on cars parked at my food co-op that say, "Think Globally, Act Locally."

Why—why do even dropout lefties insist that I have to think globally? After all, how can I think globally without thinking whatever the media tells me to think? Capitalists in China have revived the tradition of keeping lapdogs. Howard Johnson is moving into Chile. Arafat's wife wears Chanel suits. That's what happens when I try to think globally.

Or else this: I'm watching a news program about drought in the Sudan; I see closeups of babies with flies clinging to their eyelids, a woman with legs thinner than my arm; I begin crying. At the same time, I am horribly aware that I am not looking at real people—just dots on a TV screen. I feel violated by those images; they are a kind of pornography. Why is this starving woman in my living room? She's there because her image is so powerful I cannot turn away; I'm stuck on my sofa, gaping at her, until the next commercial comes on (or, in the case of PBS, the next corporate logo). Her image is not being used to inspire me to volunteer as a relief worker, it's being used to deliver me to a corporate sponsor. And that I find obscene.

Thinking globally is bullshit. It's like the old joke: A man says, "I let my wife take care of all the small details, but in our family, I'm the one who makes the big decisions. For instance, my wife picked our house and decided how to invest our money. But I'm the one who decides whether or not we'll recognize China." Too many of us think like that man. We imagine ourselves to be mini-nations, each trying desperately to formulate a position on China, South Africa, and NAFTA. And yet, when we flush the toilet, we have no idea where our shit goes. When we walk past a man huddled on the street, half the time we don't even see him. We're so dazzled by the so-called global situation, that we ignore what's next door, what's in the next room, what's right in front of us.

Listen: Jesus didn't have to watch CNN to find out about the leper colonies; he didn't question whether feeding the hungry would lead to an economic slow-down. His media was his own eyes and ears. He thought spiritually and acted locally. Same goes for Buddha, Gandhi, Martin Luther King, Jr., Joan of Arc, and all the rest.

By now, maybe you're saying, "Okay, fine, the news media sucks, but it can also do a lot of good. Am I supposed to tune out the horrors that are happening in Eastern Europe, Central America, and Africa? Isn't it important to read the paper just to act as a witness—to know about what's happening in the world? Because if enough people know, surely we will do something? Isn't it better to try to think globally than to turn a blind eye on those who suffer?"

Yes, you're right. The news media has tremendous power. If *60 Minutes* does a story on a dangerous nuclear plant, it's likely that the plant will get shut down. And when a politician knows his actions are being broadcast live to millions, his behavior may change for the better. But is that the only kind of power we can have? Are we only able to gather our information from CNN, NBC, and PBS; that is, from Ted Turner, G.E., and Mobil?

Take responsibility for your own news. Join political groups that keep you abreast of current legislation and help you figure out what to do about it. Make Working Assets (workingassets.com) your phone provider—they give you updates about the misdeeds of companies and congresspeople, and they also provide you with phone numbers so you can call in and voice your opinion. If you have a friend who's a media junkie, get your information from him or her—that means that only one of you has to spend hours in front of the tube to figure out what's going on. Get yourself put on E-mail lists that keep you up-to-date about your favorite issues. Read history books.

Most important, realize that everything you choose to do—helping out a friend instead of blowing her off, biking instead of driving, eating beans instead of steak, using baking soda instead of Clorox, buying used instead of new, living in a mixed neighborhood instead of a homogeneous suburb, sharing what you have instead of hoarding it—everything you do is a political act. You can join the revolution without even leaving your house. In fact, as far as I'm concerned, that's where the revolution begins.

THERAPY ZOMBIES WALK THE EARTH

They start as ordinary messed-up people. Then they decide to get help. That's when the real trouble starts.

MEET JACKIE *

HI GUYS. DO YOU WANT SOME ICED TEA? WOW, WHAT A COOL HAIR CUT, MARY. WHERE'D YOU GET IT?

* NOT A REAL PERSON. I SWEAR.

MONTHS LATER.

JACKIE, WE'RE WORRIED ABOUT YOU. YOU'RE SO THIN. AND YOU SAY THAT YOU'VE BEEN SLEEPING IN JAGS....

THINGS HAVE BEEN BAD EVER SINCE I DROPPED OUT OF GRAD SCHOOL. I'M SO CONFUSED. I'M GOING TO START THERAPY. I'VE NEVER TRIED IT BEFORE.

MORE MONTHS LATER.

YES. I'M DOING SO MUCH BETTER NOW THAT I UNDERSTAND HOW MY FAMILY SCREWED ME UP. MY PARENTS WOULD NEVER LISTEN TO ME. IN THIRD GRADE, I WAS NAMED BEST SPELLER, BUT THEY DIDN'T EVEN COME TO THE CEREMONY. IT'S BEEN THAT WAY MY WHOLE LIFE. BUT NOW I'M LEARNING ASK FOR WHAT I WANT. ... WHAT? DINNER AT YOUR HOUSE? THIS WEEK? OK.

AFTER DINNER...

SO THEN, UM.... HEY, IS SOMETHING WRONG?

I'M UPSET ACTUALLY

YOU, YOU, YOU. I'VE BEEN STANDING HERE ALL NIGHT WAITING FOR YOU TO VALID- ATE ME.

DO YOU CARE THAT I JUST GOT A PROMOTION? WHAT WAS YOUR RESPONSE JUST NOW WHEN I TOLD YOU THAT I WAS MADE MANAGER OF THE STORE? YOU SAID, "WOW, WE SHOULD HIRE YOU TO DO THE FLOWERS FOR OUR WEDDING." SO IMMEDIATELY WE WERE TALKING ABOUT YOU INSTEAD OF ME. ALL YOU WANT TO TALK ABOUT IS YOUR LIFE WITH RICH AND YOUR ART GRANT. WHAT AM I TO YOU — SOME KIND OF REJECT WHO DROPPED OUT ART SCHOOL AND CAN'T GET A DATE? WELL, THAT'S NOT WHAT I AM, MARY, AND I'M SICK OF THIS.

THAT ISN'T FAIR. I MEAN, I BROUGHT UP THE WEDDING BECAUSE I THOUGHT IT WOULD BE FUN TO WORK WITH YOU. I WAS JUST TRYING TO BE NICE. WHAT SHOULD I HAVE SAID?

THERE WERE A LOT OF THINGS YOU COULD HAVE SAID AND DONE. LIKE YOU NEVER EVEN CAME TO SEE MY PAINTINGS WHEN THEY WERE UP AT THE ZONE CAFE.

WHAT? YOU NEVER TOLD ME THEY WERE THERE.

YOU NEVER ASKED.

AN HOUR LATER

HEY, I GOT SOME ICE CREAM FOR YOU GUYS ON MY WAY HOME. WHERE'S JACKIE?

SHE LEFT. SHE SAYS I'M SELF-CENTERED AND THAT I HAVEN'T BEEN FULFILLING HER NEEDS AS A FRIEND.

SHE JUST STARTED THERAPY, RIGHT? DON'T SWEAT IT. SHE'S JUST GOING THROUGH THAT CONFRONTING STAGE -- DEALING WITH ALL HER SUBMERGED RAGE. AND NOW THAT SHE'S EXPERIENCED THE PERFECT RELATIONSHIP -- WITH A PERSON WHO'S PAID TO SYMPATHIZE WITH HER -- NONE OF HER FRIENDS SEEM GOOD ENOUGH.

YEAH. I GUESS MAYBE.

IT'S NOT SO SIMPLE. I MEAN, THERE WAS SOME TRUTH IN WHAT SHE SAID. I SHOULD BE MORE ENTHUSIASTIC ABOUT HER JOB AT THE FLORIST SHOP. AND I PROBABLY DO TALK ABOUT OUR WEDDING TOO MUCH.

WHAT? YOU'RE GUILTY OF THOUGHT CRIMES NOW? MARY, YOU DON'T ALWAYS HAVE TO THINK GOOD THOUGHTS ABOUT PEOPLE. AND OUR WEDDING? WE'RE GETTING MARRIED IN OUR DRIVEWAY.

YEAH, YOU'RE RIGHT. IT WAS REALLY WEIRD. SHE KEPT ACCUSING ME OF BEING "INSENSITIVE" IN THESE INSANE WAYS. SHE WAS FURIOUS THAT I TOLD TED SHE'D QUIT ART SCHOOL. FOR SOME REASON, SHE DECIDED THAT WAS WHY HE DIDN'T WANT TO GO OUT WITH HER. THEN WHEN I TRIED TO REASON WITH HER -- I SAID HE PROBABLY DIDN'T WANT TO GO OUT WITH ANYONE RIGHT NOW -- SHE BURST INTO TEARS. SHE SAID I WAS BELITTLING HER THE WAY HER PARENTS USED TO.

NO, I DON'T UNDERSTAND. YOU TOLD HIM I DROPPED OUT OF ART SCHOOL. WHY DIDN'T YOU EXPLAIN THAT I'VE HAD TWO SHOWS SINCE THEN? YOU'RE REALLY INSENSITIVE.

LOOK, I NEVER SAID THE WORDS "DROPPED OUT." ANYWAY, THIS IS RIDICULOUS. HE WOULDN'T CARE IF YOU WERE GEORGIA O'KEEFE. THE FACT IS, HE'S STILL OBSESSED WITH HIS OLD GIRLFRIEND. ARE YOU GOING TO BLAME THAT ON ME TOO?

SHE'S WORKED OUT ALL THESE INTRICATE THEORIES TO BLAME ME FOR EVERYTHING THAT'S WRONG IN HER LIFE. THE TRUTH IS, SHE'S PROBABLY MAD AT ME FOR GETTING MARRIED -- AFTER ALL, I'M ONE OF HER OLDEST FRIENDS. SHE PROBABLY FEELS ABANDONNED.

WHAT I'D LIKE TO KNOW IS WHAT THE SHRINK IS DOING. I MEAN, IF JACKIE SAYS, "I CAN'T GET A DATE BECAUSE OF MY EVIL FRIEND MARY," DOES THE SHRINK EVER SAY, "THIS HAS NOTHING TO DO WITH MARY"?

I DON'T THINK SO. IN FACT, I BET THE SHRINK IS ENCOURAGING HER TO CONFRONT ME. THERE'S SOMETHING STAGED ABOUT HER ANGER -- AS IF SHE'S PLANNED IT OUT AHEAD OF TIME.

49

SHE KEEPS TELLING ME I'M NOT FULFILLING HER "NEEDS." LIKE, IN ORDER TO REMAIN HER FRIEND, I'LL ALWAYS HAVE TO BE ON MY BEST BEHAVIOR. BUT THAT'S NOT REAL FRIENDSHIP....

MAYBE THIS IS JUST A PHASE SHE'S GOING THROUGH.

SIX MONTHS LATER.

JACKIE! I DIDN'T KNOW YOU SHOPPED HERE.

YEAH, WELL, I JUST MOVED. I GOT SICK OF THOSE ROOMMATES. I GUESS YOU AND RICH GOT MARRIED, HUH?

I JUST SAW JACKIE. IT WAS SO AWKWARD -- LIKE RUNNING INTO AN OLD BOYFRIEND. I WISH WE COULD BE CLOSE AGAIN, BUT I KNOW IT'LL NEVER HAPPEN. I GUESS SHE'D SAY THAT I WANT TO FORCE HER TO STAY THE WAY SHE USED TO BE. I CAN'T HELP IT, THOUGH. I MISS HER – I MISS THE OLD, NICE JACKIE SO MUCH!

DISCLAIMER:

I'M SURE MOST PEOPLE CAN BENEFIT FROM THERAPY. I KNOW I DID. I SAW A SOCIAL WORKER FOR A WHILE WHEN I WAS GOING THROUGH A MAJOR HEALTH PROBLEM, AND SHE HELPED ME TO COPE WITH MY ILLNESS AND DEAL WITH THE MEDICAL ESTABLISH-MENT. HOWEVER, EVEN THROUGH SHE WAS A DARNED GOOD SHRINK, THERE WAS STILL SOMETHING ABOUT THE WHOLE PROCESS OF SHRINKAGE THAT DISTURBED ME. TO WIT: SHE DISCOURAGED ME WHENEVER I TRIED TO PUT MYSELF IN SOMEONE ELSE'S SHOES OR WHEN I TRIED TO UNDERSTAND THE FEELINGS OF SOMEONE WHO ANNOYED ME. IS EMPATHY JUST ANOTHER DEFENSE? DO WE REALLY NEED TO INDULGE ALL OUR ANGERS AND RESENTMENTS?

Taking the Cure

How I Went on a Quest Out West and Sort of Healed My Psyche

What do you do when a serious relationship breaks up? How to heal the heart? Several years ago, after my then live-in boyfriend moved out, I took my cue from nineteenth-century novels: travel. Will Ladislaw, Lily Bart, Isabel Archer would split town for months or years when disappointed in love. The fresh air of the Alps put roses in their pallid cheeks. The wines of Paris taught them to laugh again.

This being the nineties, however, I could only take a week and a half off. And the Alps? Well, staying in a chalet just didn't fit my budget. But I could afford the Alps-like splendor of Santa Fe, with its healing springs, New Age comfort food, and heady high altitude, and I had a friend there whose floor I could sleep on. And my Santa Fe friend just happened to be one of my favorite people in the world.

She and I used to be roommates when we lived in Boston; back then, she was a hetero-sexual named Mina. Upon moving to Santa Fe, she became gay and changed her name to Simon, though I don't think the two things are connected. Mina—whoops—Simon produces Tarot card-

like drawings and paintings by night; by day she makes breads and decorates wedding cakes at an upscale bakery. For me, Simon is something of a role model: She lives in contented self-sufficiency, knows her herbs, and can be happy in or out of a relationship.

Even before I had decided exactly where I would go on my trip or how I would get there, I convinced my downstairs neighbors Max and Marcus to come along. Luckily Max—a Libra with strong organizational skills—took charge. Once we'd agreed on the Santa Fe plan (my neighbors know and love Simon, too), Max found ultra-cheap tickets for us all.

Yes sir, those tickets were cheap—and there was a reason. The flight was scheduled for ten hours in the air (that's not counting the two hour-long stopovers). I kept wondering, How can it take ten hours to fly to Sante Fe when it's only five hours to the West Coast? Is the plane going to taxi the whole way?

Well, as it turned out, the airline sleazebags hadn't told us that in addition to Columbus and Phoenix, there would also be a layover in Las Vegas—that extra stop was what accounted for the mystery "air time." So we suffered through four ascents and descents in an assortment of planes, but the payoff was four visits from the beverage trolley, complete with packets of "ball park" peanuts that supplied our protein for the day.

Once in Albuquerque, we secured our rental car-a trendy jeep, featuring four-wheel drive so we could barrel through the snowstorm that developed just as we arrived. After some confusion, we found Simon's place. She has her own teensy house, a faux-adobe bunker that she's turned into a showplace by painting a jungle scene on the walls of the bedroom.

Day one in Santa Fe: we waded through the snow to visit points of interest around town. I knew that Santa Fe would be full of Southwestern stuff, but I hadn't been prepared for adobe overload. I mean, every friggin' building, from the hotels to the liquor stores to the pizza joints, is a one-story box made of clay and rough-hewn beams (or an imitation thereof). The unrelenting adobeness can get annoying: for instance, the town's plaza—lined with boutiques—has the contrived quaintness of a Disney theme park. However, when you look at the buildings from far away, you realize it's a good thing that they hug the ground like low-rider cars: that way, they never block out the magnificent view of violet mountains and big sky.

Day two dawned sunny and snow-meltingly warm, so we headed out to Chimayo, a Mexican-flavored Catholic church nestled in a small town that had the best gift shop I've ever experienced: 3-D Jesuses, St. Jude refrigerator magnets, Santeria candles, inexplicable postcards. The church itself is ancient—but I was too busy experiencing its majesty to read the historical markers and find out exactly how ancient it is.

You walk into a crumbling foyer adorned with velvet paintings of Jesus, and then find yourself in a stucco chapel that smells of wet dirt, candle smoke, and the slimy secrets at the center of the earth. If you want to, you can write your wish on a piece of paper and drop it into a box—at the next church service, the priest will ask Jesus to grant all the wishes that have come in that week. Yes, this is Catholicism with a payoff. At Chimayo, no one's ashamed to make specific demands from God or to expect results from their prayers. Two rooms are hung with homemade shrines and petitions to Jesus and St. Jude: Por favor, Señor, ayudame; God protect our family in the coming year; help Michael get a job. Whenever one of these prayers is granted, the supplicants return to Chimayo to hang even more stuff on the walls. They cram the church full of tokens of their thanks: notes, crutches, amateur art, plastic flowers, plaques.

Best of all, you can bottle the healing powers of Chimayo and take them home with you: There's a hole in one of the floors filled with the magic dirt, which you can collect and use in your rituals or put inside your amulets. But don't be a hog—a sign asks that you limit yourself to one container per family.

I could feel the power of Chimayo—its mad, unintended vibe of something close to blasphemy. The church is not a monument to God. It is a monument to pain. Chimayo celebrates the weird, sexy sanctity of suffering, the agonies that destroy our egos and make Christs of us all. Crutches—grimy around the armrests—line one wall. False legs and arms hang like meat from the ceiling. Two-dollar candles burn inside glasses covered with pictures; the smoke blackens the saints, and the wax congeals into what looks like some kind of bodily excretion, cum or snot or tears; the flames glow softly, flickering with little whispers.

Bodily fluids rolled into balls of wax are burning in this shrine. Sin turned holy. Tears and tears and tears. My whole life was lucky up until the past few years. Then I lost things I never imagined I'd lose: my father, an ovary, a boyfriend, my idea of myself as someone blessed and healthy. And through it all, I think I've learned to understand pain the way the Catholics do. These scars on my stomach look beautiful to me now, like the glimmering tracks of a blind snail across my skin.

During the next few days, we zoomed around, absorbing as much scenery as we could. One morning, Simon took us over to posh Canyon Road. This is a sort of adobe version of Edgartown in Martha's Vineyard—galleries, boutiques, and trendy restaurants. But while the Edgartown tourists wear stupid corduroy pants with little whales embroidered on them, the Santa Fe tourists parade around in fur parkas and globular turquoise jewelry. The Southwestern art was generally horrible and we did our best to ignore it. We preferred to ogle the expensive homes, with their perfectly weathered balconies and walled-in courtyards.

Snow still lingered on the ground, especially up in the mountains where we wanted to go hiking. Marcus and I lacked proper footwear, so one day we cruised the Santa Fe strip until we found a Kmart. I bought a twenty-dollar pair of "fashion" hiking boots, made by Chinese wage slaves (guilt, guilt, guilt) who had glued together polyester, nylon, and rubber into an enchilada-like structure. The effect was very macho, very pro-hiker-girl, and I wore the boots proudly.

Now that we had fashionable footwear, we only needed one more accessory to achieve that rugged Southwestern look: a mountain. The next day we drove about an hour away, to Tent Rocks, where we found all the mountains we could want—mountains close enough to climb, mountains far away to provide a scenic backdrop, mountains in the middle-dis-

tance, all of them baking under a blue sky that seared our eyes.

Once parked, we headed off on a trail that led us through twisty, turny catacombs made of rock. The wind had carved out holes and passages in the soft cliffs. As we walked along, we kept passing stone pillars that had been sculpted by wind and weather into giant bowling pins. Or not bowling pins, exactly. More like fat men with tiny heads.

We climbed until we reached the peak of one mountain and stood huffing and puffing in the sudden silence. From this vantage point, we could see how the stone bowling pins crowded all around the base of our mountain, some of them rising a hundred feet or so into the air. Because of the surrealistic design of the rocks and all the earth tones, the View seemed very 1970s. Specifically, it reminded me of one of those tripped-out Yes album covers. How embarrassing.

We kept following our path along the ridge of the mountain. But the path, well, it had gone from being

a slushy trench through the snow to a halfhearted collection of footprints. And suddenly we realized that we were following the tracks of two people and their dog. Who knew where this little group had been heading? Our trail might lead back to the road, but then again, it might also lead deeper into the mountains. My hiking boots had been absorbing water steadily and were now bloated up, like sodden diapers. I couldn't bear the thought of getting lost and having to hike for hours in these foot diapers. But not wanting to add to the mood of despair in our group, I trudged along silently.

Soon the path dipped downward and, oh joy, we realized we weren't lost after all. We found our Jeep and made it back to Santa Fe by late afternoon, where—still muddy and wet—we wolfed down greasy Mexican food.

Mostly what we did in Santa Fe, though, was hang out. When the weather was too cold for hiking, or we didn't have anywhere to go in the evening, we would expand our conversation to fill up the drowsy hours. We developed a different type of hanging out tailored to each moment in the day. In the afternoon, we'd write postcards, nap, talk. At night, we'd play cards, play pool, make drinks, talk some more, listen to music. And when we woke up, we'd sip coffee and discuss our plans for the day, our hopes and dreams.

"Should we boil more water," Max would say.

"Ohmygod!" Marcus would exclaim from the other side of the room, where he was leafing through a book, "Are the pictures in here real?"

"Yeah," Simon would laugh. "They're real. I got that book at a flea market. If you flip to the end, you can see this guy with six legs."

"So, but, what are we going to do today?" I'd say, ever the goal-oriented one.

"No, no, the question is, should I make more coffee?" Max would say. And the conversation would continue for another hour without any resolution, or even boiled water.

I discovered something about myself on this trip: I'm terrible at hanging out. The thing is, I'd *like* to be happy just listening to music and talking for hours. But I'm too aware of my life dripping away, too aware of all the activities I "should" be doing.

When I was a kid, the voice-over at the beginning of a certain soap opera used to scare the shit out of me. "Like grains of sand through the hourglass, so are the days of our lives," a man's voice would pronounce. He sounded so weary and disillusioned, as if he wanted to warn ten-year-old me that growing up would only lead to disaster. As if he expected me, through sheer force of will, to stop those grains of sand from falling. But how could I? In ninth grade,

Kansas's "Dust in the Wind" could send me into a similar terror about time: that line about how everything lasts only for a moment brought tears to my eyes.

Sometime after college, I convinced myself that I *could* hold onto those vanishing moments. If only I spent my time constructively, it would somehow continue to be mine, even after it was gone. I followed elaborate exercise regimens; I wrote every day for several hours; I drew; I took guitar lessons; I tried to teach myself German by reading a bilingual edition of Wittgenstein.

I became particularly compulsive about writing: This was the activity that most contributed to the illusion that I was storing away my moments instead of squandering them. After all, what is a piece of writing but a message from yourself now to yourself in the future? Dear Future Self: This is what it was like. The trouble is, when you write—especially when you get compulsive about writing every single day no matter what—you end up missing a lot. You're too busy recording your moments to be in them fully.

For the past ten years, I trained myself to become a writer; now I am trying to untrain myself. Simon, Max, and Marcus had a lot to teach me about this. They knew how to taste the lusciousness of time passing, to float along on the river of moments. They knew how to sit outside in the winter sun with a cup of tea—just sit there without wanting to go anywhere else. They knew how to talk in desultory sentences as we drove around, dazed by the bright blue of the sky, letting the scenery fill up the silences.

In Sante Fe, I apprenticed as a floater. I'm still learning.

A week into our trip, we took off for Las Vegas—which turned out to be about eleven hours away. We made it there in one very long day of eating Fig Newtons, asking each other questions from the *Yes & Know* book of seventies trivia, listening to bad rock 'n' roll (the only kind available on the radio), and trying to figure out what all the knobs on the dashboard did. At 10:00 P.M. we rolled down a big hill and saw the lights of the city spread before us; the desert floor looked as if it had been covered in miles of gold lamé.

We headed straight for Bob Stupak's Vegas World, which had been recommended by several friends. The hotel/casino did not disappoint. The complex was easy to spot, thanks to an "astro tower" that rises perhaps two hundred feet into the air; the tower, still under construction, looks like an ashtray on stilts. As we approached the entrance to the casino, I nearly cried at the beauty of it all: "rocket-flame" lights overhead, giant dice designs underfoot, an "astro car" parked out front. When we walked through the door, we all stopped short, overwhelmed by the dark cavern of kitsch that confronted us. Because of the mirrors on the walls and ceiling, the place seemed as vast as outer space—a new kind of outer space with planets-and-stardust carpeting, rows of beeping slot-machine androids, and see-thru-plastic pillars full of bubbling water. Above us hovered a life-size astronaut, a near-life-size space station, and a few planets. We explored the lobby, able to say nothing to each other but, "Oh my God, oh my God, oh my God."

It seemed as if Mr. Stupak hadn't updated any of the decor since 1972. I mean, who would even think to do a NASA-theme casino these days? Twenty years ago, Americans looked to space as an exciting frontier; now it just seems like a sinkhole for government funds, a shabby suburb of Earth full of space junk and sicko aliens who stick probes up your butt. But at Bob Stupak's, space is still vast and promising.

Unfortunately, when we tried to register at the hotel, we found we'd been shut out by seniors. Busloads and busloads of seniors pile into Stupak's as part of some sort of vacation package—leaving no vacancies for scoffing hipsters such as ourselves. So we climbed back into our Jeep and cruised the strip to pick another hotel.

We'd been driving since 9:00 in the morning, it was now after 11:00, and our defenses were down. When we saw the thirty-foot-high clown gesturing for us to pull into Circus Circus, what could we do but obey? The casino/hotel—sculpted of pink-and-white something so it looks like a circus tent—is spangled with lights. The rows of lightbulbs that cover the entrance and the buildings front canopy click on and off with a loud electric sound, a Frankenstein heartbeat. We went inside and signed up for the cheapest rooms, in the "Manor" two blocks away—this turned out to be a glorified motel.

Next morning we paid a mere three bucks each for Circus Circus's all-you-can-eat breakfast bar. You shuffle along, pick up a massive plate, and then are herded past piles of food-blintzes, scrambled eggs, cereal, bacon, muffins, bagels, cut-up fruit, dough-nuts, ham, coffee cake. In Vegas, we ate only two meals—all-you-can-eat breakfasts and all-you-can-eat dinners, keeping our food expenses down to about ten dollars per day.

After breakfast, we began walking along The Strip, popping into casino/compounds long enough to soak up the different vibe of each one—actually they all offered pretty much the same clanging horde of slot machines. The average casino-goer everywhere seemed to be an elderly woman in a jogging suit sucking on her cancer stick as she fed quarters into a slot machine. Even when she hit the jackpot and the machine spat out a huge pile of coins, her expression—boredom? resignation?—didn't change. She just scooped the coins into a little plastic bucket and began feeding them back into the machine.

We *loved* Treasure Island. One minute you're shuffling along the Las Vegas sidewalk—seedy characters, vacant lots, chintzy tourist shops. The next minute you find yourself in a Moorish village by the sea. The sidewalk turns into a wooden bridge, and beside you flows a body of toilet-bowl-blue water in which a pirate ship and British schooner lie half-submerged. Cliffs rise in the air. A barbarous and picturesque people have made their dwelling in the cliffs. They've hung hand-loomed rugs, silver plates, and bundles of garlic cloves along their balconies. Their tumbled dwellings seem to be constructed out of rough-hewn wood, stained glass, and even human bones—though it all looks suspiciously like molded fiberglass.

A sign informs you that the ships do battle every hour and a half. Marcus wanted desperately to hang around and see this, but we got sucked along by the traffic flow and were whisked away from the ships, into the casino, past some life-size skeletons that moved and wisecracked when we came near, up an escalator surmounted by a bank of video screens on which a giant face appeared and began talking to specific people in the crowd ("Hey, you, blond lady in the black sweater—wipe that grin off your face"), through a long passageway, and into the Mirage. This latter casino, in case you haven't guessed, is owned by the same folks who brought you Treasure Island—and they make sure that you visit both. All the escalators and moving walkways and monorails shuttle you between one casino and the other.

We shuffled along through the tropical rain forest lobby of the Mirage (which is complete with palm trees, streams, and rocks) and found ourselves following signs for the white tigers. It turns out these poor animals live behind glass, across from the Mirage gift store, and serve as walking-roaring-shitting advertisements for the Siegfried and Roy magic act. Above the White Tiger Viewing Area hang several monitors; these continually play a video about how Siegfried and Roy care so much about the earth that they saved the white tigers from extinction. Of course, if you're a white tiger living out your days in a molded concrete pit inside a casino, well, extinction starts to look pretty good.

Siegfried and Roy. Siegfried and Roy. They hovered over the white tigers, they glared at us with Teutonic grimness from billboards, they posed in magazines. There's even a statue of S&R along The Strip—two giant heads with big eyes and long flowing hair; usually Siegfried and Roy look kind

of mean, but the statue makes them seem as cute as Care Bears or My Little Ponies. At some point, Marcus spotted a picture of S&R from fifteen years ago. "Hey," he said, "they looked older then than they do now." It was true. The 1980s S&R had weather-beaten faces and squinty eyes; these days, S&R's skin stretches across their cheekbones so tightly that they look almost like aliens—possibly the result of face peels and lifts the pair must have had.

Weeks after I'd come home from this trip, I ran into my friend Michael at a party. He laid a frightening fairy tale on me. Roy has been replaced. Yes, that's right. Years ago, the real Roy contracted AIDS. Siegfried—not willing to give up the million-dollar magic act—recruited Roy's cousin to replace the ailing Roy. After several rounds of plastic surgery, the impostor was ready. According to Michael, the "Roy" you see on stage these days never talks—lest his voice give him away.

An hour or so later, we returned to Treasure Island so we could watch the sea battle. As we waited, people crowded onto the wooden bridge until it was packed tight. Finally, some college-kid-type actors in costumes leaped onto the ships, and the canned music started to swell. The British captain proclaimed something like, "Ahoy, that blasted brigand yonder seems to be challenging us. We will fire a warning shot." Only the actor wasn't actually saying anything; he was lip-synching, because the dialogue—like the music—was piped in by invisible speakers.

The ships began "firing" at each other. When a ship was "hit" it emitted jets of fire and plumes of smoke, and the actors would dive into the water. The whole performance seemed to be an excuse for these explosions, which erupted only a few feet away from the audience. Balls of fire shot out of the pirate ship as it sunk, and "treasure" went flying everywhere. When the show ended, the ships moved with mechanical solemnity back into their original positions, and the crowd filed away into the lights and clatter of the Las Vegas street—which now seemed quiet and dark in comparison.

At about eight o'clock, we went back to the motel and collapsed. I had blisters on my toes and my legs ached. It wasn't just the walking that had exhausted us—it was the barrage of bleating machines, crowds, exploding ships, talking statues, loud carpets. All of these stimuli came at us so fast, faster than we could absorb them. Now we lay on the beds in my motel room, gnawing on some bread left over from our 5:00 all-you-can-eat bacchanal at the gay-nineties-riverboat-theme casino. We tried to get up the energy to play cards, but couldn't.

The next day, we gadded about—hitting the Liberace Museum and other points of interest. It wasn't until late afternoon that we made it back to The Strip. This time, we planned to attack the newer end of Las Vegas Boulevard, where—instead of no-nonsense casinos—you find the family fun-and-gambling theme parks.

It was dark by the time we made it to MGM Grand, a hulking building that seems to melt into the sky. At one end looms a deco sphinx—you enter the building by walking between its massive paws.

Once you pass through the paws, you find yourself (incongruously) in Oz. Before us spread a poppy field, and life-size Dorothy, Scarecrow, et al., and behind them an Emerald City the size of a Kentucky Fried Chicken building.

I have a very uneven metabolism—sometimes I'm so tired I can barely sit up and other times my face flushes and I turn into a hyper-active kid. The minute I entered Oz, my metabolism kicked into overdrive. I ran around, admiring the giant mushrooms, the ice crystals, the sky that dawned and set every twenty minutes, the life-size Wizard of Oz who talked to you as he floated upward in his balloon. We missed the best parts of Oz—you have to pay five dollars to walk along the yellow brick road and get inside Emerald City—but I didn't care. Even the free parts of Oz were so overwhelming that I could hardly contain myself.

But soon enough my manic happiness turned to paranoia. Marcus reached over and plucked one of the plastic poppies a few feet from the yellow brick road.

"Don't," I hissed. "Give that to me. Jesus. You can't walk around carrying that." I snatched the poppy out of his hand and stowed it in my bag. "They have cops in places like this. Haven't you heard of the Disney cops and the Disney jail? It's probably just the same here."

MGM Grand wore us out. Nonetheless, we wended our way to Luxor. You're clearly not meant to walk to Luxor; we had to weave our way through several parking lots and traffic islands to get there. But we knew we were headed in the right direction when we saw a statue of Ramses near a traffic light; and then, under the palm trees in a parking lot, an obelisk covered with hieroglyphs. Green lines of light blinked across the face of the obelisk and lit the sky above of us with snot-colored lightning. We had stumbled across Luxor's famous laser display.

Inside the hotel, we wandered along hushed halls beside a river—yes, a faux Nile flows through the football-field-size lobby of Luxor. For three bucks you can climb onto a barge and ride around on the mini-Nile. You float past "ruins" as a tour guide gives you what is supposed to be a fanciful synopsis of Egyptian history; however, the spiel ends up being an offensive plug for the hotel. Considering that in Las Vegas three dollars will buy you enough food to make you vomit, the barge ride was a bad deal. All of Luxor was one fat rip-off we decided as we sat in the Tiki Bar, nursing our swollen feet.

After some liquid refreshment, we managed to start walking again—retracing our steps past MGM Grand. When we neared Caesars Palace, we couldn't resist lying down on the moving walkway; so we were whisked into Forum Shops at Caesars Palace on this mechanical flying carpet. Inside the Forum Shops (an ancient-Rome-theme mall), we milled about for a few minutes before we noticed that everyone else seemed to be gathering around a huge fountain. In the middle of the fountain sat a life-size Bacchus, and four other gods stood around its perimeter.

"Laser show," "laser show," we heard the crowd whisper. And sure enough, the ceiling above the fountain suddenly lit up with whirling stars, splotches of color. And then...and then...one of the statues began to move. What seemed to be stone was actually some kind of mobile plastic. The statue opened its white eyes, moved its arms, gave a little speech. Then the other statues woke up and spoke. Finally, Bacchus's chair began spinning around and he laughed in a mechanical bark and then welcomed us to Caesar's Palace and the shops in the Forum mall. At the same time, the fountain spewed colored water and lasers played all over the ceiling.

Had I suddenly come upon this display in Boston, I would have been awed. But the awe receptors in my brain were totally burned out. As the gods wiggled and pontificated, I just stood there, numb.

When the whole thing was over, we stumbled away. None of us could think of anything to say, except for Beavis and Butthead remarks like, "Well, that was cool," and "Yeah, it was okay, except nothing exploded."

I was burned out. "Please, God, no more talking statues, no more giant tiki heads, no more laser shows," I prayed to myself. "Just let me make it back to the motel in peace." The motel room—with its deep carpet, framed pictures of balloons, and impersonal hush—had begun to seem like a sensory deprivation booth after all of this.

But my silent pleas were not to be granted. For— as we dragged along the sidewalk past the Mirage— mist swirled around our feet. It seemed to be rising off the fake waterfall in front of the casino.

"Oh," Max said in a dead-tired voice. "The steam's coming from that Volcano." He pointed to a fiberglass mountain that loomed in the midst of the fake Amazon in front of the Mirage. The volcano rumbled and a jet of fire shot out of its mouth.

"Let's stay and watch," Marcus said.

"*No!*" Max and I both said at once.

Back in the motel room, we collapsed on the floor, even more exhausted than we had been the night before. You know how sometimes when you're watching MTV, the images flip so fast you can barely see them? We'd been subjected to a 3-D version of that for twelve hours. It made me feel passive, and oddly *clean*—as if my brain had been running hot for hours and now all the grit and clotted oil and old grease had burned off.

In our weakened state, all we could do was flip through the channels on TV. Normally, television jangles my nerves; it's too loud, too hyper, too happy. But now the world inside the television seemed to move in slo-mo.

One of the channels on our Circus Circus television offered us a variety of pay-per-view movies, all of them sucky and some of them X-rated. Seeing that list of porno movies—*Breast in the West, Charlie's Anals, Oral Report*—reminded me of my ex-boyfriend, the one who'd moved out of my apartment, the one I was on this trip to forget.

I could just imagine what it would be like if he and I were staying in this motel room together. He would have begged me to let him watch one of the porno movies and I would have said, "I'm not your mother. Go ahead."

Then he would have jumped up and down on the bed in glee. "Yeah! We can watch *Breast in the West*! We can drink malt liquor!"

And I would have gone along with this. I played the tolerant, nondoctrinaire feminist when I was

with him—I refused to get offended. Instead, I piled his porn magazines neatly on his bureau when he left them on the floor.

Why did I put up with all this? Partly because it all seemed sort of like a joke at the time, and partly because he saw himself as a victim of the modern media environment, unable to filter out the mouth-watering images that assaulted him.

We had big fights over the TV in our apartment. I needed it there for my work, since I sometimes review TV shows and videos. He claimed that the presence of the TV—even when it was turned off—tortured him. He said he was like an alcoholic and the TV was liquor that I was leaving in front of him. Eventually we came up with a compromise: We locked the TV inside a cabinet. I would bolt the cabinet doors closed with a combination lock—so that he wouldn't be able to watch hours of TV whenever I left the house. But after a while, he found that he could crack the doors open, turn on the TV, and watch a sliver of the screen. Just that sliver of video could seduce him with its narcotic images, could silence whatever he wanted to silence in his own head.

My ex-boyfriend would have loved Vegas, and hated it, too. He would have railed against the American need for overstimulation even as he fed coins into a slot machine. He would have dragged me to a live nude-girl show and would have enjoyed it so much that I would have started laughing along with him (a wary, anxious laugh—I only realize that now), and then we would have gone back to the motel and screwed our brains out, high on the sickness, the slickness, the commodified sex all around us. I'm amazed now how that kind of behavior seemed normal at the time.

The next morning, Max and Marcus and I went to the swank all-you-can-eat breakfast buffet at the Tropicana—more expensive than Circus Circus, but worth it because the food wasn't disgusting. We stuffed our coats and backpacks with bagels, muffins, fruit—hoarding food to get us through the eleven-hour drive back to Santa Fe. Or maybe our drive would take even longer than that. We planned to veer off the interstate and travel on Historic Route 66 (as it's now called), to see the sights along that neglected highway.

So after breakfast, we piled into the Pathfinder and drove up, up, up, out of the desert. We stopped at Hoover Dam to use the bathrooms, and to lean over the railing and gaze at the dry concrete valley hundreds of feet below us.

After the dam, we drove on the interstate a few hours, agonizing about whether or not we really should detour onto Route 66—we were afraid that if we took 66 we wouldn't be able to make it to Santa Fe in one day. But finally, somewhere after Concrete, Arizona, we took the plunge.

Whew! What a difference. Instead of whistling through the blank desert at seventy miles per hour, we proceeded at a stately fifty-five mph, passing through one small town after another. We glimpsed jack-legged houses, cafés with faded signs, ranches, gas stations with 1940s pumps, lonely motels.

At one point we stopped for coffee at a diner. There was only one other car in the parking lot. Inside the restaurant, two Native American women

leaned toward each other at a table, talking in desultory sentences. An old man sat at the counter reading the paper. The waitress wandered over to us and painstakingly poured the coffee. These people seemed to have been sitting in the same places all day. Time moved like syrup here, like the thick and sweet Log Cabin that sat on every table. When we left, the screen door slap-slap-slapped behind us.

The farther we traveled on Route 66, the more tentative the road became. Finally it narrowed down to one thin strip of asphalt, crumbling away at the edges, so you couldn't quite tell where the asphalt left off and the dirt began. This part of 66 wasn't even on the map—the road had officially ended a few miles back. Around us stretched tan fields of wild grass, and beyond that the purple mountains majesty.

"Whats that?" Marcus said, pointing into the fields.

"What? What?" Max said. He pulled the jeep to a stop, right in the middle of the road.

"Deer," Marcus said, and then I noticed the herd that blended into the blond grass. They had their heads up, watching us. We sat for a moment, going nowhere on Route 66. The sun was setting over the mountains in front of us, turning the clouds orange and pink.

And then Marcus cracked open the door to get out. The deer startled, turned tail, and floated over the grass. The three of us climbed out of the car and stood, blinking and disoriented, on the road. Our shadows stretched behind us. A few birds swooped over us, wings rustling like newspaper pages.

Where was I? I didn't know exactly. All I knew was that I'd left Las Vegas that morning. I'd left the city of flashing signs burning through the night, live-nude dancing girls, store-bought sins, all you can eat, loose slots, grimacing clowns.

I felt like I'd lived in Vegas for the past two years. But now all of sudden—without knowing quite how it happened—I'd found myself inthis strange place, standing in the limpid half-light of evening on the crumbling asphalt of a road less traveled. The hush of the desert around me was profound. Here, the world knew how to hold its breath. Here, the world waited to see what I would do next.

FRIENDS & FAMILY

It's telling that MCI picked *friends and family* to be the words that characterized its zillion-dollar ad campaign, rather than the older, more-standard term *family and friends*. Apparently, even Corporate America acknowledges that friends come first these days.

In this rootless age—when people so often move away or grow away from their relatives—a family is no longer something we're born into. We have to make it ourselves. My own family includes my mom, my sister, and my boyfriend, and also an ex-boyfriend and his girlfriend, the guy I own my house with and his boyfriend, several members and ex-members of my writing group, my mom's friends, my sister's boyfriend, and a bunch of ex-housemates.

This salad-bar approach to kinship has its advantages. It's portable and it's flexible. But it also can be an awfully big pain in the butt. Keeping your patchwork family knit together takes a lot of energy, especially because it's unclear how close we are to friends and what we owe them.

Most of us assume that our sexual relationships need rules. We're in the habit of talking with our lovers about how close we'll be, what we'll share. Unfortunately, friends rarely have such conversations. But what if, say, you agreed with one friend that you would help each other out in times of sickness? What if you agreed with another friend that you would tolerate each other during emotional collapses? Wouldn't you feel more secure, surer of your safety net?

I've actually had a few such conversations with my friends. And these pals, along with many others, have proved themselves to be family many times over. They've nursed me through illness, lent me money, offered me three different free cars, housed me, and fed me lots of soup. I guess none of it compares to what, say, my mom has done for me—those long hours of labor and the potty training and all—but I'm still pretty darn grateful.

Babes in the Woods

Some Thoughts on Reproduction

Once upon a time, a little girl was wandering through the woods when she stumbled over something soft and spiky. At first she thought it was a hedgehog, but when she picked it up, it turned out to be a grubby elf. He'd gotten himself tangled up in a set of those nonbiodegradable plastic rings that hold beer cans in a six-pack.

"Well," the elf said, "don't just stare at me. Get me out of this thing."

She gently pried the rings off of his neck and his legs. He had a gash across his stomach, and so she cleaned him with her spit, and then took a Band-Aid off her own knee to cover up his wound.

"By the law of the forest," the elf said, "I now owe you one wish."

The girl didn't even hesitate. "I want equal rights for everyone in the world."

The elf rolled his eyes. "You think I can do a 'whole world' wish? I'm just a forest elf, and I've got a pretty limited repertoire here. A mansion— you could have a mansion. Or bigger boobs. Or—I know—how about a prince?"

"No!" the girl said. "None of that is good enough. I want to be treated like a man!"

"Are you sure that's what you want?" The elf fixed her with a stern eye.

"Can you do it? Can you make everyone think I'm a man?"

The elf rubbed his face. "I hate granting wishes. You know, at some point, you're going to regret this wish, and then what happens? You'll probably slap me with a lawsuit."

"No, I won't. I promise," the girl said.

"Tell you what. I'll make the spell reversible. If ever you want to undo it, curtsy three times toward the East," he instructed, and then he scurried off into the forest.

It was all as the elf promised. When the girl walked home, her mother glanced at her, and then began laughing raucously. "James, James!" the mother said. "Why do you wear a skirt and a kerchief on your head?"

"It was a prank they played on me. Oh mother, it was horrible. They made me pretend to be a girl."

"You poor thing," she said. "Let me find you some breeches."

And from that day, she wore pants and boots.

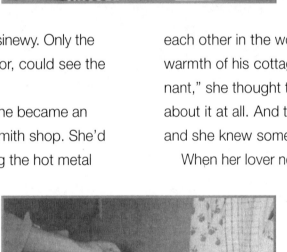

Everyone who looked at her saw a boy. On her smooth soft face, they imagined the first pricks of stubble. Her budding breasts they saw as muscles. Her coltish legs appeared to be sinewy. Only the girl, looking at herself in the mirror, could see the truth.

When she turned eighteen, she became an apprentice in her father's blacksmith shop. She'd never been happier—hammering the hot metal and soothing the horses as they stood waiting, discussing crops with the men who came in, and drinking spiced wine with her father when the work was done.

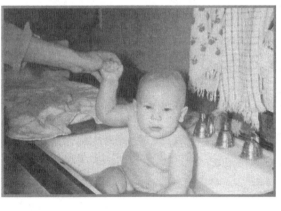

In time, she fell in love with a farmer who lived in the next town. Whenever he came in with his old mare, she turned away—not wanting to stare at his thick, beautiful arms or hear his laugh. She knew she couldn't have him, and her heart ached. But still, she did not undo the spell. For she loved her life as a man more than she loved any man.

The farmer began appearing at the shop every few days. He lingered there and struck up conversations with the girl. He brought her goats' milk and eggs. Why does he want to be my friend so badly? the girl thought.

One day he followed her on some errand. When they were out in the quiet of the country, he said, "You are so delicate and beautiful!"

The girl's voice quavered with fright. "So you know? You can see me as I really am?"

"I knew you were like me, a lover of men, from the moment I met you."

The girl and the farmer carried on clandestinely, meeting each other in the woods and sometimes in the warmth of his cottage. Maybe I can't get pregnant," she thought to herself, when she thought about it at all. And then one day she woke up and she knew something was growing inside her.

When her lover noticed her new belly, he was delighted. "You're filling out. You're growing into a man," he said.

At the first pangs of birth, she ran away and hid in the woods. What doctor would deliver a baby from a man? The girl would have to do it herself. She made herself a nest out of straw and ate willow bark to ease the pain. Her muscles were strong from swinging a hammer all day, and within a few hours, she managed to push the baby out.

The infant lay curled up and tangled in his cord, like that elf had so many years ago. The girl cleaned him off and cut him free. The baby screamed, grasping the air with his miniature fists. She lay him on her stomach and he quieted, his eyes roving all around without ever fixing on hers.

"Oh no," she said to herself, "oh no," for she had just now understood that the baby, too, saw her as a man. Soon he would begin needing milk, but instead of feeling soft breasts when he groped her body, he'd find hair and muscles and useless little nipples. And so, the girl stood up, put her breeches back on, and— pulling the fabric as wide as it would go—tried her best to curtsy.

For months, I've been working on this essay about reproduction. I started it as a political screed, as a confession, as a rant. Nothing seemed right. How could I explain my feelings about having kids? Some of my fears made sense—my phobia about falling into the ranks of single mothers, more than 50 percent of whom live below the poverty line; my reluctance to add to the population problem; my suspicion that it's difficult to get a male partner to do his half of the child—rearing work. But I have other fears, too, fears that I find hard to explain.

It was only when I tried a new approach— writing about my feelings in the form of a fairy tale—that I began to understand that I've been carrying around a certain superstition for years. I half-believe that if I act too womanly—and especially if I bear a baby—I will be punished.

Why do I believe this? I grew up during the early years of feminism, when the only freedom women could imagine was men's freedom. I was ten years old when *Ms.* magazine first appeared; its founder, Gloria Steinem, exemplified the ballsy new way for women to be. Steinem hid her Playboy-bunny face behind huge glasses, resisted marriage, and devoted her life to political causes instead of kids. All the other women I admired during my impressionable years—Charlie's Angels, Virginia Woolf, Bat Girl, Billie Jean King, Jane Goodall—were also unfettered by men and children.

We Americans believe in two contradictory ideas: equality and meritocracy. These two ideas got mixed up in my young mind— and I'm sure in many other girls' minds—and I secretly believed that to deserve equal rights, I would have to "prove" that I was as powerful and independent as any man. I entered college as a biology major because I was convinced that the humanities and arts were for sissies. I was determined to show the world I could be as proficient in the sciences as any man; if first-year chemistry hadn't been excruciatingly dull, I might be working in some lab today.

But I continued to try to prove myself in other ways. I wanted so badly to have a man's life that I began to hate everything female about myself—I threw all my energy into my career, dressed butch, acted tough. Sometimes I thought about how I could have kids without giving up my life as a man. When I was about twenty-five, the solution seemed obvious: I'd find a guy who wanted to be a wife. I'd earn the money—since I understood how to cope in the business world but I didn't have a clue how to raise a child—and my husband would be the soft-spoken guy who adored kids and, by the way, was an excellent cook. Well, I've had boyfriends who were genuine feminists, who could whip up a gourmet meal or calm a two-year-old. But none of them wanted to be wives, and I don't blame them. A few years later, I came up with Plan B. Ditch the nuclear family, because two working people—or one—cannot have a kid without a lot of juggling

and sacrifice. What if five adults vowed to live in the same house, share finances, and raise kids together? Then nobody would have to be the wife.

But I only entertained these thoughts in the most speculative way. I never seriously planned to have kids. In fact, I joked that I wanted my tubes tied or my vestigial womb cut out. I just couldn't imagine myself as a mother. By the time I was in my late twenties, I'd settled into my man's life: running a business, traveling around, spending long stretches of time working alone. I was happy with this life, even more so because I was finally learning what I wanted from my romantic relationships. It was something strange and elusive, something rarely depicted in movies or in books or on TV, but real nonetheless: an erotically charged equality. My own private name for it is "love in drag," and it involves a recognition by both parties that gender is only a mask. I'd discovered that plenty of guys craved it as much as I did. It seemed that, finally, I was learning how to love a man without giving up my own masculinity.

Our lives unfold like fairy tales. Whenever we venture into the woods, an elf may appear to grant our wish. The trouble is—as every children's story teaches—those wishes turn out to be curses. I was the girl who wanted to be a man. I was the girl who wished her womb would go away. And I got my wish—more or less. Soon after I turned thirty, one of my ovaries ballooned to the size of a grapefruit. The doctor who removed it told me that I'd had a rare growth of borderline malignancy; he suggested I have a complete hysterectomy within a year or so.

For a month—the time it took me to find another doctor—I went around believing I was about to lose my reproductive organs. I, who never cared, was besieged by feelings, swept by storms of tears. Most of all, I mourned my genitals in a way that had nothing to do with gender. After all, they were the only genitals I'd ever known. For this reason, I now favor the term castration rather than hysterectomy. It's more primitive, more evocative of the way I felt back then. And the term is unisex—reminding us that the loss of ovaries can be just as devastating as the loss of testicles. Certainly I felt as terrified as any man about the prospect of becoming a eunuch, of losing my sexual power and perhaps an essential part of my personality. What surprised me was that I also grieved as a woman. Motherhood was the wild card I'd always held and never used. I had the power to wake up any day and decide, "I'm going to conceive a baby." The thought of losing this power was unspeakably sad, like losing the only magic spell I knew how to cast.

Even as I mourned for my womb, I began to understand why I'd always been so ambivalent about motherhood. In a science fiction movie called *They Live*, the protagonist puts on special sunglasses and is able to glimpse the true messages behind advertisements. Underneath the bikini-clad women on billboards he sees hidden commands like Obey, Consume, and Submit. During my ovarian hell, I felt like I was wearing a pair of those glasses. The commands and threats that our society uses to control women were suddenly obvious. In the billboards, in the comments of people around me, in newspaper articles, I could see the real messages: Have a Baby or You're Going to Get Cancer; If You Can't Procreate, You're No Good to Us; Soon You'll Be Too Old to Breed, and Then You'll Come Crawling Back and Admit Your Entire Life As a Career Woman Has Been a Sham.

My doctor had urged me to have kids as soon as possible and then to get "cleaned out"—have my ovary and uterus removed. My then-boyfriend warned me that, despite his feminist values, he wanted to be with a woman who could bear his babies. My mother freaked and urged me to procreate immediately. And suddenly I noticed all the articles in magazines that I'd managed to tune out for years: news stories about how women up their chances of cancer by putting off childbirth; cautionary tales about career women who wait too long to breed, and then bitterly regret their decision. These news stories may contain seeds of truth, but their truth is fertilized with piles of bullshit. In the late

eighties, Gloria Steinem—the woman who'd always said her family of friends was enough, that she didn't need kids—began visiting doctors in New York. Rumor had it that Steinem was seeing fertility specialists; finally, America's high-profile feminist had realized she would never be happy until she had a baby. In fact, Steinem was consulting doctors because she had breast cancer.

I knew that our culture tries to make childless women feel like shit, but in my weakened state, I no longer had the power to resist the propaganda. I began to question my old values. I'd always wanted to change the world, write brilliant books, learn to love a man as an equal partner—but none of these accomplishments could ever be as satisfying as motherhood. My stupid bohemian dreams had blinded me to the most simple of facts: I was biologically destined to have babies. And yet, even my weakest moments, the thought of actually going ahead and having a kid scared the hell out of me.

Luckily, my fertility angst passed. I chose not to have the hysterectomy. I got rid of the sexist doctor; I broke up with Mr. Biological Children; my mother calmed down and became very supportive. Now, three years after my near-castration, I find myself returning to the same questions that I dallied with in my twenties. How can a woman struggle toward equality with the extra weight of a baby on her back? How can a woman—knowing that the average marriage lasts about seven years—be sure she won't end up raising her kid alone? But these questions seem different to me now. I used to imagine them shouted out, like the slogans you scream at a march. Now I hear them posed in a weary voice, conundrums that cannot be solved or answered.

For I'm beginning to recognize that underneath the feminist's question—who's going to raise the kids?—lies the central question of our time. We now expect parents to help support their children for at least eighteen years, to provide a stable home life, and lots of one-on-one time. And yet, adults demand the freedom to change their sexual partners, to work, and to relocate when they can't find a job—actually, work isn't a choice anymore, now that most families depend on two incomes. So how do you balance the needs of adults and kids? Our culture offers only one solution: money.

Have you noticed that in the last ten years, kids have become a luxury item? Those scented perfume ads show mothers nuzzling babies, fathers cradling a child. The favorite prop in catalogues has become an infant; a few years ago, my friend Bob was walking around in swim trunks, baby daughter in his arms, and everybody began commenting, "Oh my God, you look like you just stepped out of a J. Crew catalogue."

Can a happy adult raise a happy child—for cheap? Lately, I've been returning to the ideal I had long ago, that children should be raised by many adults rather than just one or two. Through most of history, extra child care was built into the family—aunts and uncles, grandparents, and parents lived together and shared the work and joy of kids. Now people pay for baby-sitting and day

care, if they can. But the extended family provided a lot of other benefits that are hard to buy—home-cooked meals, fellowship, entertainment, safety, the convenience of group living.

How in a rootless culture—when Grandma lives in Miami, your ex-husband lives in Cleveland, and your Mom in New York—can we revive the extended family? Many parents I've talked to belong to an informal support group or play group. All across this country, mothers have woven a web or traded favors and shared labor; but that web is fragile. How can we weave a stronger safety net? One solution is to honor parenthood in all its forms and to invent new forms. What if single people could "adopt" children who already have parents? Then I could legally become the second mother of my friend's baby. This arrangement might satisfy harried parents and also people like me, who'd rather be the indulgent auntie than a full-time mom. What if families could "adopt" each other; make a decision to live nearby and to share cars and meals and yards? What if adults lived together in a honeycomb of houses and apartments— singles, couples, parents, and older people all banding together to form an impromptu tribe?

Then we might stop believing in this fairy tale, the fairy tale of no-money-down minivans, kids clad in perfect Baby Gap outfits, fortresses in the suburbs, and women who manage to hold down jobs and be full-time moms, too, without cracking up. Let's wake up from the advertisers' dream, look around, and figure out how to glue together the shambles of the American family.

Note:

All baby pictures used in this spread were found in the trash.

THANK YOU FOR

According to Les U. Knight, founder of the Voluntary Human Extinction Movement, the best thing we can do for the planet is to abstain from reproduction. I interviewed him on his back porch in Portland, Oregon, about the finer points of his philosophy.

Your basic ideas are what?
The Voluntary Human Extinction Movement is based on the idea that we all live long, happy lives, but we don't add to the population problem. A lot of the members have already reproduced—well, actually, there aren't any new members, because there is no organization. There's not need for it. It's a movement.

Extinction Fun Facts

- On an average day in 1990, the world's population increased by 260,000.

- Forty thousand children die of malnutrition every day.

- You may believe that if you have two children, you aren't adding to the world's population. Not so. Since most people now live for several generations, we don't simply "replace" ourselves with children. To do that, we'd have to die off immediately after breeding.

So the people who have joined the movement don't have kids for planetary reasons?
Well, everybody has their own reasons. But for vehement volunteers its mostly a deep ecological motivation.

So you wouldn't go around killing off people, though?
That wouldn't do the job. There are a quarter of a million more people born than die every day, so you'd be a very busy person trying to kill off a quarter of a million a day. And that would just hold the population even. Whereas if you were able to prevent a quarter of a million conceptions, well, you'd really have something there. Since half the births of the planet are unwanted…

Where did you get that statistic?
The UN says that between a third and half of the babies born today, their parents would not have had them if they had a choice. In America where we have a little better estimates; it's about 58 percent unintended, and about half of those are aborted.

So a lot of kids in America just aren't wanted.
Yeah, well, they want them afterwards. My daughter's baby is two years old, and he was unintended but wanted.

Tell me about your personal reproductive history.
When I got out of the military in 1970 I became interested in the environment, maybe because it looked like something I could take care of. And it all came down to one thing: human activity The more I looked into it, the more I looked at population growth. ZPG [zero population growth] had just started. The Population Bomb came out in sixty-eight. I realized we needed a moratorium on births. No births for twenty-one years. And then I thought, Why bother to stop this moratorium?

We have to ask ourselves, "Why should we continue the human race?" I really haven't found a good reason for that.

NOT BREEDING

In light of the tens of thousands of children who die of preventable causes every day and the millions of species going extinct because of our increase, I don't think the intentional creation of one more human being by anyone anywhere is justified.

Hey, wait, you stopped your personal history at 1970.

Well, I got a vasectomy because I wasn't about to have an accidental human. And then I met a woman with a daughter who was five years old, and we all started living together. I became her father. I never was against children; in fact, I teach school. I really enjoy working with children. And so I became her father. She's on her own now; she's twenty-two.

How old are the kids you teach?

I teach high school. Substitute teach.

So you're committed to the kids who are already here.

Oh yes. That's what we have to do—take care of the people who are here. If people want to be parents, there are plenty of kids who need parents.

Maybe this is really obvious, but it seems to me that politicians are always saying "We're doing this for the sake of the children." But it seems to me that when you dig underneath the surface, America hates children. Have you had that feeling?

I sure have. That hatred comes out of fear. People are afraid of them. It's getting even worse with the media hype about gangs and so on, and playing up the idea that teenagers are about to kill everybody. And so people hate them and then they do things to them like adjudicate them and remand them to the adult court for petty offenses. Give mandatory sentencing guidelines.

The best example that we dislike children is how much we go on and on about how much we like them.

So what is the practical platform for your organization?

The motto says it all: May we live long and die out. It's a wish, not a command. Not everybody should get sterilized. It's far too complex for women. And not all men need vasectomies—only sexually active heterosexuals.

It seems like this is such a touchy subject. Do you get hate mail?

No. The only time there's any problem is when there's some kind of misunderstanding. Because when people think of human extinction, what usually clicks in their brain first is killing, death, suicide. This demonstrates the blind spot that we have. We don't think about preventing conception.

You don't get any flak?

When you have a position as dismissable as voluntary human extinction—you want to persuade everybody on the planet to stop reproducing...

You're not much of a threat.

Exactly.

Tell me about your newsletter.

I wanted it to be positive. There are misanthropes who say, "Yeah, let's get rid of this human race, were just a bunch of evil people." Or another one is that we suffer so much that we should go. Well, I don't agree with that.,We're not evil and my life is great—I'm not suffering so much.

It's true that we're incompatible with the biosphere and we should go extinct. We are growing like some kind of malignant tissue on this healthy organism. But we are better than a cancer. We have love and we can decide consciously that we want to stop.

Fun Facts about Les U. Knight

He holds croquet parties in his backyard every Sunday.

He publishes other newsletters under other names.

In addition to a croquet green, his backyard contains a "mystery spot"— a homemade roadside attraction. It's difficult to describe the mystery spot, but let me just say this: you climb down a ladder and find yourself in an underground cavern, among the artifacts of a lost civilization.

Each person who is not created here in North America is the same as about thirty-three East Indians not being created; and in terms of energy consumption alone, one of us [North Americans] is the same as five-hundred Ethiopians. So when we choose not to have another [North American] human being—it's not just a baby we're having, it's an entire adult—we're saving a tremendous amount of resources.

So you put out the newsletter—what else?
There isn't really any need for action, though almost all volunteers do something in addition. There's a volunteer on the *Sea Shepherd* working to preserve marine wildlife; there's another working to halt French testing of nuclear weapons.

Once you decide not to reproduce you have a lot of time. In fact, the person on the *Sea Shepherd*—his marriage almost broke up when he decided he wasn't going to reproduce because of the earth. His wife always wanted a baby. But now she's just as strong about it as he is. And they both realize that he wouldn't be out on that ship getting in the face of the Norwegian Navy if they had kids.

Where are they now? *SFWP Reprint Edition.* The Voluntary Human Extinction Movement is still around. Find them online at www.vhemt.org.

Three Women and No Baby

An Interview with Some Broads Who Decided Not to Breed

One day I invited three women over to my house to discuss their decision not to have kids. Susan, who's forty-six, and Nadine, fifty-two, showed up first. The two friends stumbled into my apartment, laughing so hard that they had to lean on each other. They were speaking in fake hillbilly accents, which apparently is part of some elaborate game they play whenever they're together. "Ya see, Pagan," Susan said in her drawl, "we didn't have kids because we prefer to act like kids ourselves." Susan is an artist; Nadine, a writer and therapist.

Later that afternoon Karen—a thirty-three-year old gay lawyer who works to protect the rights of the disabled—dropped in.

Nadine, you said that your role models—of women who chose to be childless—come from the gay community.

Nadine: I was part of a spiritual community that was based on Native American practices, so there were a lot

Susan and Nadine, posing for me

of gay women drawn to it. They all had very fine minds. They weren't afraid of their minds, so that was interesting for me to be around.

Are you saying that women are afraid of their minds?

Nadine: Well, silent. Or women who just sort of get married and are a little Vacant. I was married when I was twenty-one, so I was part of that. I became a little glazed over.

How long did you stay married?

Nadine: About a year [laughs]. But these gay women were great, because they thought life was okay. You know, there are women in their fifties and sixties who are just having a wonderful time for themselves— they're either partnered or not, but they don't have kids.

But I always wanted to have kids, so I went through a lot of heartache.

Did you make a decision not to have kids?

Nadine: Not like Susan. It happened to me, and I had to keep surrendering and making peace with it. I suppose I could have gone out and gotten inseminated, but I felt [I had to have kids] within a relationship. So there were several crises along the way. When I was thirty-seven, there was a major relationship that didn't work, and that was a heartbreak, because my social programming was so strong to do this. And then I was in another relationship when I was forty-two. So at that time I went through a big passage of knowing that if I didn't [have kids] with this person, it wasn't going to happen. We broke up, and a part of me was shattered—I hadn't just lost the relationship, I'd lost this program that I'd been brought up with. Everything my mother had told me. And my mother died at the same time. She realized that I wasn't going to produce grandchildren for her.

So you must have felt guilty.

Nadine: Not really. She was depressed anyway. But it was one more thing that wasn't going to manifest for her. I think my sister and I didn't want kids because my mother was not a happy woman and hadn't lived out any of her dreams.

So at forty-two, I realized I had a big job to do on my head. I got my own apartment. Of course I'd done that before. But it was like, "This time I'm really going to stand on my own two feet." So it was a real beginning. A lot of my forties was building this very exciting network of travel and people.

Do you feel like you were dealing with the social programming or genuine biological feelings?

Nadine: I think both. I did have a strong biological urge. My work now is around motherhood—I mean my work

writing, teaching, and with clients. There are lots of children out there in the world who need to be nurtured.

Susan: What do you think you would have given up if you had kids?

Nadine: I have and have had a lot of solitude.

Has it been good?

Nadine: Fabulous.

What about you, Susan?

Susan: Freedom is the first thing that comes to mind. I've always regarded it as a choice between children and work. Intellectually, I don't believe that's true, but psychologically it's always felt like one or the other. I could not have done the work I've done if I'd had kids—I get very involved with people I love. If I had kids, I would be too full with them. The solitude is a big thing—I need a lot of it.

Again [like Nadine], I see my mother as having given up her life for children. I don't have a positive role model for a mother.

But there's another piece for me here. I couldn't have kids since I was twenty. I stopped producing estrogen. I'm sure that lack of estrogen has an affect on me. I know there are a lot of women who can't have kids and are tortured by it. But I've never been tortured by it. I always thought I was lucky.

So you think the lack of estrogen did something to you mentally?

Susan: There is a physiological relationship. I used to think the biological clock was a media invention. But now I think there is something to it, because I've seen friends of mine of a certain age—like thirty-five to forty-five—in this desperation about having kids. It could be that you know the time is finite. But it does seem like there's a chemical component.

Karen: I'm in that range of time where it could happen. But it probably couldn't happen—because I'm a lesbian—unless I was very proactive. It's hard to figure out what feelings come from wanting to fit in in a way you just don't if you're gay in a straight society. I look around at my friends who are having children, and I think it's something I'd like to do. And it also seems like it's part of a package that's pretty attractive. I live on the edge financially. I'm alone in a lot of ways—which I like and I've chosen. But sometimes I just want to be normal.

Susan: That's something I've felt. There were two times when I wanted to have kids. One was when I stopped running groups. [Susan used to be a group therapist.] For about a month after that, I'd wistfully look at women with baby carriages. I thought I just wanted to be a housewife. That lasted a month, until I went on to the next thing. And the second time was when I was getting divorced from my first husband. A lot of my friends were having kids. I would go to these people's houses and feel this incredible longing for a family. Once I broke up with Robert, however, that passed. It's almost embarrassing how blatant it has been. Whenever I've thought about having kids, it's to fill a hole. I wanted to use kids to keep me from feeling something. But I've been driven, because I have that vacancy that I need to fill with a lot of meaning. And it's good because it pushes me.

Do you think kids would fill that hole?

Susan: Kids might have made a difference. People have told me that having kids stops them from having to ask questions about the meaning of life. I'm not sure I want those questions stopped, however.

Nadine: There's something about building a family and a community. I've been with a man for two years now, and we just bought a house together. We're both too old to have kids, and that's great. But prior to being with him, I was satisfied because I had a community. A lot of intimacy needs got met by that—other single women.

Well, Karen and Susan said that, too. It's not kids—it's the web that you want.

Nadine: This thing about how you carve out a life that's authentic, it's a big question. Even buying a house with someone—we're not even married, but it's like, "Eeek." How do you avoid feeling like you're in some suburban movie? Or if you get married, how do you make it your marriage?

Susan: I was thinking about what you said, Karen, about wanting to be normal. Which is something I've always longed for. Logically, if I look at that lifestyle, I really don't want it. But I think my generation escaped a lot of that pressure because we were on the cusp of feminism. It seemed like a very valid choice not to have kids. My husband and I have been living on the edge—financially and stressfully—but it's been worth it. We put together a conference on the arts and humanities policy agendas for a national information infrastructure, and we bankrupted ourselves. Both of us had no income for two years. But it's amazing how we managed, and I don't regret it.

Nadine: In one of Joseph Campbell's texts, he talks about the path of security. It's so easy to fill that space with family and marriage. The other is so on-the-edge. I certainly like that feeling of freedom. But there is a knife edge to it.

Susan: We get to be a lot more self-indulgent! We get out of bed when we have to be at work—which for both of us is, um, plastic. And if we want, we can have our evening in the morning.

Do you think if you're creative it fills the need to create a human life?

Susan: I feel like it does, but a lot of people don't. The canvas becomes a universe over which I have complete control—and that's fine. The trouble is, kids tend to get that energy from their parents. Wanting to control what you create is full of problems when what you create is a living being.

Karen: I was just thinking about the fact that it takes courage to create your life instead of stepping into a life where the plot structure has already been developed for you. Having children, to me, is one of a variety of creative projects that you could immerse yourself in. I don't think most people think of it that way. You could do that or you could create your life in another way.

Nadine: It's so exciting. I remember when I was thirty-seven and I decided to take this long cross-country trip to decide if I wanted to be with Joe. I thought, If you go back and marry this guy, that's okay. And if you don't, that's okay, too. That was a real feeling of "I choose to create this." It was a feeling of my life as a book. That this is my story.

ON-THE-FLY-FAMiLY

how one group balances adults' and kids' needs

For many years, I've hung out with John—mostly we see each other at parties. With his easy laugh, wholesome good looks, and vintage slacks from thrift shops, John could have just stepped out of an old sitcom. Maybe he's the young father who lives next door to the Partridge Family, Maybe he stands in his driveway every Saturday to enjoy the perfect weather of an America still innocent of ozone-layer damage, where the sun bounces off the chrome of his gas guzz/er. Maybe he has two kids and a wife with bullet-shaped breasts.

Actually, as I got to know John, I learned that he is a father, of sorts, and that he strongly believes in his own version of family values. However, the family John belongs to is the kind that would have gotten drummed out of most sixties suburbs. Three kids. Three houses. A band of adults linked by the ever-shifting ties of gay and straight romantic love, friendship, and roommate-dom. (See diagram.)

I knew that John was helping to raise two of the kids with his lover (who's the biological father) and the kids' mother. This arrangement intrigued me, but i was shy about asking for all the details.

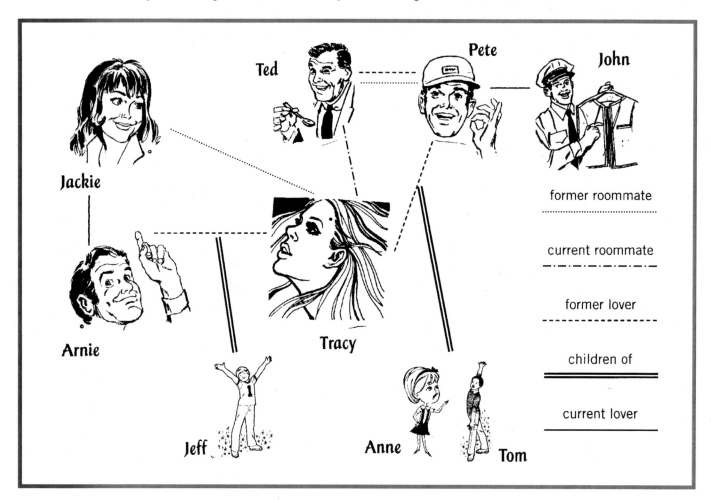

Note: Everyone in the family except John asked that I change their names. For some crazy reason,
they didn't want all their personal gossip published in a book.

And then this book came along and I had the perfect excuse. So I went over to the house that John shares with his boyfriend, Pete, and where the fourteen-year-old Anne and seventeen-year-old Tom live part-time. Anne, who was about to leave for a weekend trip, spent the whole time on the phone. Tom—who insisted that his real name was Nick Blinko—was hanging with a posse of pals. I interviewed John, Pete, and Tom— whoops, I mean Nick—about how their family evolved and how it works.

Tell me—who's in your family?

Pete: Well, let's start at the beginning. I fled upstate New York. I was seventeen, and my mother said I either had to go into the service or stay in school. My sister stepped in at the last second and gave me this opportunity to live down here [in Boston]. She saw I was going into the Air Force, and she was like…This was seventy-six.

I was totally closeted, from out in the boonies where there's no images of gay people at all. And then here I was dumped in the middle of the South End. So I got here and her husband—I mean, her mate—Al, they're thinking I need to get screwed. They fixed me up with the daughter of the owner of the garbage-truck yard. A black woman way older than me. I was supposed to go out with her and go to bed with her. So anyway, that kind of stuff was going on.

john

Around then, I met Tracy. She's about fifteen years older than me. She kind of took me under her wing— to live in her house— and we started this relationship. She said, "I don't want to be married." I felt like, Wow, I can get in this relationship with this woman and have this cover. So I moved in with her in Dorchester. She had Jeff already. He was about five years old. She was divorced from Arnie.

Tracy offered to have a baby with me. Here was this opportunity. I was twenty when Tom was born. After Tom was born, I started to explore the rest of myself—the rock clubs and the 1270 [a mellow gay club]. I met John at that time, in 1982.

This was totally bumming Tracy out. When I told her I was gay, she was encouraging me. But whenever I started to do it, she flipped.

John: So anyway, Pete and me met at the 1270 in 1982. At that point, we were so far apart culturally. I was a middle-class suburban kid. We saw each other a couple times but we were too different . . .

Pete: When you say "saw" you mean "went to bed." It sounds like you mean I saw you across the room.

John: Okay, okay, so I went to France, and we fell out of touch. But then I had an acid trip. *[Ed's note: At this point in the conversation, John went into a long description of the trip. I've spared you the details]* That's when I realized Pete was the one. But I didn't know how to find him.

Pete: I was still living in the same place.

John: So in '86, I had spent the night with this guy and I wasn't into it at all. And then in the morning I realized, Oh my God, this is Pete's neighborhood. I remembered where his house was. So I went up and rang the bell. Pete comes down in his white tank top. This was four years since we'd had any contact. I had met Tom, but now he was seven. And Anne had been born. I started hanging out with them nonstop. Tracy couldn't deal with my interloping.

pete

Pete: It was pretty clear we were into it. Tracy was liberal in theory, but the reality…I came home one day and found she had locked me out, with no warning at all. But then, later, she became completely amicable. I got a room in an apartment a few blocks away—an apartment with John, Ted, and me. Ted was a lover I had when John was away in France. Now Ted's living with Tracy.

Oh my god.

Pete: Yeah, he's part of the family.

John: Oh, but there's more, Pagan. So, anyway, I had to make this decision to move in with Pete and his old lover [Ted] and that was just a stone's throw from where the kids were living with their mother. There was a lot of back and forth. Then Tracy and the kids moved in with us and Ted moved out. That lasted for about six months. It didn't work.

Pete: So Tracy moved in downstairs from us. And then she moved down the street. We've always managed to stay no more than a few blocks away. That's what's given us this flexibility. Pretty much I didn't go through any days without seeing the kids. I'd bring them to school or I'd pick them up when Tracy couldn't.

Did the kids like it?

Pete: Well, I'm sure the kids were bummed about it sometimes, but they were going to Boston public schools and they saw kids who didn't have any parents at all.

John: For the most part, they saw their parents cooperating. Myself, coming from a divorced family, I was envious of Ted and Anne. They could still feel their parents being together.

Pete: We'd [all be going out together] and we'd introduce ourselves to people, and they'd be looking at us like, "How can you all be together without ripping each others' eyes out?" We'd all go on vacation together…Now we're literally two houses away.

And then, um, remember Jeff [the kid that Tracy had with Arnie]? He kind of got lost in the shuffle. His father had been in the background. But then, when Jeff started getting out of hand, his father [Arnie] came on the scene. Arnie and Jeff moved to Delaware, where Arnie hooked up with Jackie [an old roommate of Tracy's]. They got married and moved up here. They're now living next door. Jeff moved back up here from Delaware, too.

Wait, there's somebody else…

John: Ted [Pete's ex-lover and ex-roommate]. He lives with Tracy now.

Pete: It's this constellation that's been in flux over the years. Who knows where it might go. John and I are planning to buy the place next door. Possibly there's another room for Tracy to be able to live there, too.

Tom, a.k.a. Nick Blinko, enters.

anne

How did you like how you grew up? Would you have rather grown up in a Brady Bunch family?

Nick: Not at all. Oy! That's all I have to say.

How about being able to walk between your parents' houses?

Nick: Well, I could always avoid doing things.

Pete: It was bad, bad, bad. He used it to get away with doing what he wasn't supposed to do.

What kinds of things did you get away with?

Nick: If I got grounded at one place, I'd go to the other one.

Pete: We got totally fed up by the time he'd go to the other house. He'd get grounded…

Nick: No TV.

Pete: Then he'd go to the other house and we'd cool down and the momentum would be lost. It was hard to carry through with limits. And also, Tom being the master of deception that he is…

But I feel pretty confident that they had a reasonable life. So many traditional, heterosexual couples have skeletons in the closet…

tom

Well, [referring to the animal bones that sit on the shelves and the windowsills all around the house] here the skeletons are all right out in the open.

John: Want to see our whale bone?

Marry Any Damn Thing You Want

A Queer Wedding Lets You Celebrate Your Own Version of Family Values

Gleth is a queer studies-ologist who teaches at Sarah Lawrence College. She recently finished a dissertation on wedding rituals, and has partcipated in a number of alternative marriage ceremonies. Unfortunately, she has few photos of these queer weddings—I guess everybody was so busy riding on motorcycles and figuring out what inanimate objects to marry that they forgot to grab their cameras. Perhaps this is another unique feature of queer weddings—unlike the straight versions, they are not spectator sports. But anyway, that's why the pictures included here of a gay and straight wedding party are so shoddy.

I talked to Gleth about what weddings should and could be—rituals that validate not just romantic love, but all the affiliations and ties in our lives.

What is a queer wedding, and how can people use them?

I think it's really important to distinguish between a queer wedding and a gay wedding. A gay wedding can be spectacular, but it's basically a commitment ceremony for a couple. A queer wedding, on the other hand, celebrates connections that aren't accorded the status of marriage—not only gay couplehood, but friend-ship, collaboration, ex-lover-hood, triangles, et cetera. A wedding is like a huge theme party, but since people have roles to play and there are lots of aspects to camp up, it takes more artistry. So people can use queer weddings to celebrate any damned connection they feel proud of, and to exercise their brilliance in coordinating a pageant. Also, a queer wedding isn't a marriage. No legal strings attached. In a weird way, I think of the queer wedding as a collective leap of faith.

Have you gone through a queer wedding yourself?

I've been in three weddings I'd call queer. The first was a protest called "Weddstock," a marry-in that was part of a campaign for domestic partnership bene-fits at the University of Chicago. In a lot of ways it was hard for me to get behind the idea of extending privileges to people based on their ability to get their emotional, sexual, intellectual, and financial needs met by only one other person. If anything, I think that's something that needs to be discouraged because it seems like a recipe for disaster. So the "marry-in" was also designed to celebrate liai-sons and connections that had no privilege whatsoever connected to them—a group of house-mates married one another and also a blow-up doll of Edvard Munch's "The Scream," a triad of ex-lovers chained themselves together, and I married a friend with whom I shared a weakness for married women. I had this idea that I'd put a tiny Kleenex veil on my left hand and marry it as a pledge to continue my masturbatory life for, well, life, but I had to choose.

I officiated the second queer wedding at the Univer-sity of Chicago, and more or less married myself to the entire wedding party. That one felt more sedate to me, but I did ride up the aisle on the back of a motorcycle driven by a luscious undergraduate, and officiated in a leather harness. I believe the campus paper said I needed a spanking. I wish. The third queer wedding I went to was a private divorce ceremony in a parking lot with a straight colleague of mine. We pelted each other and a third friend with rice, burned her ex's picture, and raised our glasses for a curse before smashing them. Very cathartic.

I'm intrigued by the idea that friends can be married to friends. In our culture, we pay so much attention to romantic relationships and so little attention to friendship. Are you trying to honor friendship in the way that we would honor romantic love? Or does that ritual suggest that the line between romance and friendship is blurry?

I am not so sure that the line between friendship and romance is always blurry; I think it really depends on the people involved. But I do believe that this culture has a sad dearth of rituals for entering into and exiting friendships, as well as rituals that involve the larger culture in sustaining them. It's possible that friendships are inherently more stable and thus don't need all the trappings that marriage does, given its rate of failure and misery. But I think the problem lies more with the culture of couplehood.

In this culture, you are either coupled or single— as if uncoupled people are total isolates. I think it would make coupled people a little more humble if they had to attend friendship weddings, buy presents, say congratulations. People should worry about their friendships the way they do their marriages. People should accord friends the same respect and support that they do couples. A wedding might help inaugurate that.

There is a commercial I love with a group of girls playing soccer and chanting wedding vows as they kick the soccer ball around. It's a Nike ad, and it somehow makes visible the way these girls are connected with one another, the devotion they have to one another and to the game, without reducing them to "brides." It's as if the vows they recite give their teamwork an erotic and a female dimension without humiliating them as athletes.

One of the coolest things about a wedding is that it lets two people who aren't related choose to become kin. In the gay community in particular, people have a sense of

constructing their own families out of friends, neighbors, co-workers, et cetera. Does the queer wedding have something to do with that—the idea that we can choose our own families?

Definitely, although even the word family somehow manages to subordinate the idea of chosen relationships. Perhaps Dan Quayle has ruined the word forever. Queer weddings have to do with making chosen relationships visible (if not permanent—I don't think weddings ought to produce marriages, frankly), and with allowing other people to participate in the making of a relationship among two or more people. So not only do they dramatize the idea of choosing your own kin, they make it clear how many other people's support and labor go into maintaining a relationship of any kind, and they demand that kind of witness and support for relationships beyond couplehood.

Is it a new way of declaring that someone— even a nonromantic friend—is now a part of our family?

Sure, yes, of course. But it's also a way of letting people act out, assume roles in relation to someone else's drama. I think of a queer wedding as a talent show for amateur media whores, as well as a solemn ritual. I was surprised how much I liked being a bridesmaid at my brothers straight wedding, for instance. Even though I was the fat bridesmaid with the growing-out hair in the unflattering dress, par-

ticipating in a ritual designed to totally eradicate the relationships central to my life, I still played my role with irony and finesse. I danced the chicken dance, I flirted with poor unsuspecting groomsmen, I lived out the alternate universe in which I'd been born a mall chick from Long Island.

In the queer weddings I think I was positively sublime. Grown-ups too rarely get to play pretend, and the wedding is really an adult ritual, unlike birthday parties. I think the most important thing for us as a culture to do is to get rid of marriage benefits and spousal privilege, and just have a whole bunch of weddings. In my utopia, everyone would get at least one. It beats a funeral, which everyone actually does get in one form or another. And by then its too late to enjoy being the star of the show.

BETTER HOMES

Pagan Kennedy's Living:
The Magazine for Maturing Hipsters

The curtains that you stare at as you wash the dishes, the old trunk at the foot of your bed with its worn wood grain, your toothbrush—these items are trusty props in the performance-art piece that is your life.

Unfortunately, advertisers understand this all too well. They want to make you question the parts of yourself that you express through china and glass, wool and wood. In recent years, Martha Stewart has become a towering cultural icon precisely because she embodies our fears about our homes. Are we stylish enough? Do we live as elegantly as the earth-tone-wearing yuppies at Martha's parties? Can we achieve in our own homes the beauty we see in those photos—the flowers in mad shades of pink, the golden custards in bowls coated with a mint-colored frost, the clean lines of a Shaker chair?

Let's stop letting ourselves be bullied by Martha, the slime-dripping demons who are her advertisers, and all the other purveyors of good taste. It's obscene that we allow them into our homes, the one place where we have enough privacy to experiment with our own idioms of style, to make our kind of beauty, to really enjoy the textures and colors of things—from a shiny gum wrapper to a dusty scrap of velvet.

How can you reclaim interior decorating for the left wing? Maybe the key is to remember that nothing in your house is really yours. Many of your chairs and pictures and plates belonged to somebody else before you found them; and most of your possessions will be passed on to someone else after you die. You and your fork are like lovers, brought together by circumstance and soon to be parted. Everything you own has been or will be recycled. So let's learn to love our things the way we should love people, knowing that they don't really belong to us.

House Hunt

For five years, I lived in an elephantine Victorian house on a shady street in one of the cheap neighborhoods in Boston. People walking into the place for the first time couldn't believe it: when the massive door swung open, you'd glimpse elaborately carved fireplaces, wainscotting, stained glass windows, a grand staircase, and plaster arms sticking out from the wall, a la Cocteau's *Beauty and the Beast*. The architectural details had been built by craftsmen in the eighteen hundreds. The weird artwork on the walls was supplied by our friends and by local trash cans.

For a long time, I knew I'd found what I'd been looking for: the perfect living situation. In the summer, I'd settle on the roof with a book, or hang out on the porch with my roommates, or sun myself on the fire escape; the house, designed in a more gracious period, was a honeycomb of crevices and nooks. It seemed to be made for lounging. And lounging was what all of us—the eight to ten people who inhabited the place at any time—spent most of our time doing. We formed an impromptu family—Thanksgivings together at a long table full of pot-lucked food, borrowed CDs in one anothers' rooms, even roommate incest. Incredible people passed through that house: the women architects from Texas who lovingly restored the upstairs kitchen; several rock stars; Sid and his pet pig; a massage therapist who saw clients in an extra room; a grad student who had to watch hundreds of hours, on videotape, of people talking in American Sign Language.

But by the time I turned thirty, I was sick of the downside of group-house living. I'd been burned one too many times by the Law of Roommates: good ones leave. For maybe a year, we'd have the perfect combination of people, and then someone would get a job on the West Coast and someone else would move in with a girlfriend. Every time we lost someone, we'd have to start all over on the frightening and treacherous roommate search— one wrong move and we could be stuck with a meat-grease-splattering, non-bill-paying, Pink Floyd-cranking jerk.

But even if I'd always shared the house with the best people—let's say, Jesus, Gandhi, and Mother Teresa—I would have gotten fed up. Gandhi probably would get carted off to jail all the time—very noble, Mr. Pacifist, but what about the gas bill? Jesus would invite his apostles over every night, and they'd probably leave their dirty wok in the sink. Mother Teresa would get phone calls day and night from lepers, who would treat us like her personal secretary. Even with the saintly roommates and a color-coded chore wheel, you can't change the essential nature of group living: You'll always be picking other peoples hair out of the drain—that is, you will if you ever find a moment when the bathroom is free.

Though I was fed up with overcrowded group houses, I still wanted to live in some kind of communal situation. So I began to look into co-housing. I'd learned about the idea—a more civilized, nineties version of the commune—through my food co-op newsletter. It advertised a new co-housing group in the area, people who were getting together to dream up a utopian neighborhood that would include shared gardens and dining halls, as well as apartments for singles, seniors, and families.

It's hard to say exactly what co-housing is, because it is so many things. More than 150 groups have sprung up in the U.S.—groups in different regions, with different income levels and different ideals. Some have already erected their dream neighborhoods and are looking to sell condos; others are in the planning stages. If co-housers have anything in common, it is their wish to figure out the perfect blend of private and communal space; to allow people to belong to an extended family and still be able to slink off to their own apartments; to discover a new architecture, one that fosters community spirit rather than suburban isolation.

At first glance, co-housing seemed like the perfect solution. But the more I investigated, the more I got a bad feeling about it. First of all, there's the problem of money. Most co—housers say they want to draw a diverse population, so why are many of the developments located in creamy white suburbs? Why are the price tags so high? I certainly couldn't afford the down payment on a $120,000 one-bedroom unit in a new co-housing development in the suburbs of Boston. For that kind of money, I could have bought an entire house in the ratty, rock 'n' roll neighborhood where I preferred to live. Then there was the time involved: Many co-housing groups buy a plot of land together, and then spend years deciding what, exactly, to do with it. That means endless hours of consensus meetings. Ugh, spare me. As a political activist, I was used to suffering through meetings about Central America, civil disobedience, and recycling. Now did I have to go to meetings just to find a goddamned apartment?

And, most important, I didn't want to join a community. Co-workers, ex-co-workers, ex-roommates, ex-lovers, old friends, zine publishers, fellow writers—here were so many people around whom I cared about. I already had my own haphazard yet fully functional community. I wanted to live with my friends, not a bunch of strangers.

Right around the time I gave up on co-housing, I heard about two people who'd taken matters into their own hands. An acquaintance of mine and her friend had bought a duplex together, splitting the down payment, repairs, and mortgage. Each woman ended up with her own apartment. These friends were more than co-owners; sharing the burden and joy of the house, they'd become impromptu family members.

It was Max—one of my oldest friends, and a neighbor in my beloved punk-rock suburb—who told me about the women. Their example inspired us. We looked over the agreement that they'd drafted, and soon Max and I decided to buy a duplex together, too. For us, it was a pragmatic solution. Neither of us had enough money to buy a house on our own; together, however, we might be able to find something.

And so we embarked on our real-estate odyssey. We agreed on the kind of house we wanted (a duplex with two-bedroom apartments and a backyard) and where we wanted it (the quieter sections of our rock 'n' roll neighborhood). We eased into our search by looking through the papers every Sunday and going to open houses. Later on, we got some real-estate agents to drive us around in their Jeep Cherokees and take us on power tours. I much preferred the open—house method. We didn't know what to make of those peroxided real-estate agents and they didn't know what to make of us. Usually they assumed Max and I were a couple and kept up a bubbly stream of talk about the great schools nearby, the parking, the stores. Sometimes we both had our boyfriends in tow, which drove real-estate agents into a confused silence. It was awkward for everybody.

Then Max found what seemed like the perfect real-estate agent for us. I'll call her Olga. She was a recent immigrant from Russia, had stained teeth and a heavy accent, and wore mismatched clothing. Unlike the other real estate agents, she made no effort to cover up her money lust. "You want this house?" she'd scold. "What's wrong with this house? You tell me, we'll make a deal."

One Sunday, Max dragged me along to an open house—a bedraggled, sagging place I'd noticed on my jogs through the neighborhood and thought, Who would ever buy that? We wandered through the downstairs apartment, examining the stained floors, the mustard-colored carpet, the sagging porches, the dark rooms, the furniture left by the old woman Who'd died there. It looked like the set of "Sanford & Son." But it was the first house we'd seen that fit our budget, that was the right size, and sat on a street we liked. Max—who's always been attracted to dark and cramped spaces—loved it. I thought it was awful, but agreed to come back later and see the upstairs apartment. (We hadn't been able to see it that first time because the tenants weren't ready.)

A few days later, Olga let us in. "Watch out for the cat," she yelled. "They'll be mad if the cat gets out!" We obediently followed her up the stairs and into a room with gleaming floors and varnished trim (the room I'm working in now, as a matter of fact, and it's strange to think of it then, occupied by someone else's computer, somebody else's rug and table). We toured the well-kept, sunny apartment. The tenants were obviously a yuppie couple—they had an impressive stereo setup and cream-colored living room furniture. Max and I snooped through their stuff, examining the photos that sat on a table and checking out what CDs they'd collected. Olga joined in. "Ah yes, that must be them," she commented, picking up a wedding photo. After we walked out of the house, after Olga disappeared in her economy car, I said to Max, "Let's bid on it."

Up until now, we'd been thinking of our house search as a sort of performance-art piece. Touring real estate had been a goofy way to spend our weekends. But now, now that we were getting down to business, I had a bad case of impostor syndrome. I thought we'd never be able to buy a house because the owners wouldn't take us seriously; instead of accepting our bid, they'd send back a message: "You're not fooling us. You're just kids. Why don't you get back to us when you have real jobs." So I was in shock when the owners accepted our bid.

Of course, that was only the first step. Next, Max and I began the arduous and surreal process of applying for loans. If I felt like an impostor before, now I knew I was one. We met with our first loan officer in an overly air-conditioned, deep-carpeted office; he shook our hands and then gestured for us to sit on the other side of his desk. Max and I had tried our best to look like a young professional couple, but we weren't fooling this guy. Our business suit-type clothes came from AMVETS and the Salvation Army. We'd ridden our bikes to the bank on a summer day, without deodorant. And when we spread all of our financial documents before the loan officer, we had nothing to offer but a bunch of freelance jobs. Never mind that we had an impressive amount of savings; never mind that our combined income was pretty decent. Never mind that I had just won a sizable grant from the National Endowment for the Arts. Banks don't like the self-employed.

"I need a pay stub. Don't you have any W-2s?" the loan officer kept asking. It turned out that my N.E.A. grant didn't count as income; the bank only recognized grants that paid out over three years. Hello? Hello? Reality check. How many small-business people—even people outside the arts—get that kind of long-term grant? The loan officer sorted through our collection of 1099s and forms that proved we'd been paid by clients. Finally he found a W-2 stub from one of Max's jobs. "This is good. This really helps," he said. "Why don't you have more of these?"

Max laughed. "I just happen to be on the payroll at that company. They could have easily paid me with a 1099 instead. It was just chance."

Needless to say, we were turned down for the loan.

After a few more interviews, we finally scored with a lending company in a shoddy office building—though the company wouldn't front us the full amount of the house. We had to pay the difference out of our savings.

Meanwhile, we'd run into some trouble with the owners of the house. Olga told us that they weren't willing to evict their tenants. She wanted us to agree to buy the place with the tenants in it. Our lawyer told us we'd be suckers to comply with this. After much wheedling, Max convinced Olga to give him the owners' phone number. When he finally got them on the phone, it turned out they had no idea what he was talking about. Apparently, she had fabricated the whole thing herself—probably because she was afraid that if the tenants refused to leave, the deal would be off. This taught me a valuable lesson: If you're a buyer, there is no such thing as a trustworthy real-estate agent.

*   *   *   *

So, anyway, its three years later. Needless to say, we finally managed to buy the house. We've reshingled one side of it, torn down and replaced a porch, taken out the generic suburban bushes and replaced them with poppies and columbines and wisterias. Max found an intercom

system in the trash and installed it between our two apartments; now we can buzz each other when we want to borrow garlic. We compost our kitchen scraps, collect rainwater. Max and I and our boyfriends all share one car; we find stuff for each other in the trash and go to yard sales together.

Our experiment has been a success, largely because Max and I trust each other and because we share the same values. For instance, we both have a laid-back attitude about household business. Our role models, the women who bought that duplex together, drew up an agreement—a sheaf of typewritten pages explaining how to divvy up the ownership of the house. Every time one of them puts money into repairs, they have to recalculate who owns what percentage of the house. So, for instance, if one person paid for a $5,000 roof, then her share might go up by two percent. Trying to read through the contract and figure out their system, I got dizzy. I didn't want to do all that.

To this day, Max and I have never drawn up an agreement. Instead, we decided to save our receipts and to keep track of the hours we've worked on the house; when we sell the place, we'll go through our papers and figure out who's put more into the house and what to do about it. We split all major expenses—like the cost of building a new porch. And over the years, we've also developed our own private economy of exchanged favors. It is the economy of friends, of give-and-take.

Deciding to buy a house with someone is sort of like deciding to be his blood brother. You'll become more financially and legally entangled with that person than you are with your own family members and possibly your lover. If you're going to do it, pick someone who you trust absolutely. When we bought the house, Max and I had been close friends for almost fifteen years and shared beliefs on all the major issues: communal living, environmentalism, and what kind of wood to use for a porch railing.

Sometimes I wonder what possesses people who decide to buy houses with their lovers or spouses. After all, the average marriage lasts about seven years, according to recent census statistics. If you're going to take on a thirty-year mortgage with someone, why does it have to be the person you sleep with? Moreover, lots of people—single mothers, older women, life-long bachelors—do not have the luxury of choosing to buy with a spouse. As families change and marriages become more tentative, nontraditional home-buying is going to become much more common.

Already, some developers have gotten hip to this trend and are building developments that encourage communal living. But why wait for the housing revolution? Let's work with what we've got. That's what Max and I are trying to do, anyway. Rather than building a co-housing community from the ground up, were trying to encourage it to grow organically—colonizing this neighborhood with our friends. Whenever a "For Rent" sign goes up in a window nearby, Max puts out the word. That's how his pal Patty ended up moving in across the street. And our friends Scot and Amy—attracted by the community we'd formed—moved in a few blocks away.

Of course, most of the people who live around us don't belong to our circle of friends. And that's turned out to be a joy, too. When we bought this house it was like we married into a large, crazy family. Who are our neighbors? The lady next door who signs for our packages when we're not home. The Vietnamese family across the street who blasts Muzak and who gave us all the bricks they pulled out of their yard. The kids—white, black, Asian—who come trick-or-treating on Halloween, most of them dressed in identical, store-bought Power Rangers costumes. The guy who taps maple syrup from the trees in his yard. The head-injury guy who roams the street—he can hardly talk, but most people call out, "Hi, Joe," when they see him. This little working-class neighborhood came equipped with its own sense of community, its own unspeakably strange culture.

Forget gentrification. Forget preplanned, specially built co-housing developments. There are plenty of shabby suburbs and grungy urban neighborhoods in second-rate cities all over this country. These places have a rare beauty all their own. Let's dust them off and appreciate them.

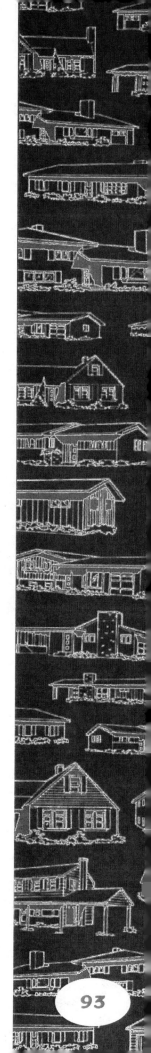

Scientist Reveals:

I LIVED INSIDE A ROBOT

TIM IN HIS TECHNO CAVERN BEING INTERVIEWED BY PAGAN. NOTE TOILET PAPER-DISPENSING ROBOT OVERHEAD.

Tim, an inventor, has been given free space by a university (which he doesn't want me to name). The cavernous room has a concrete floor and pipes running along the ceiling. It's crammed with broken industrial robots, a twenty-five-pound bag of plantains, and cubbyholes with labels on them like "earplugs" and "small metal objects." And then there are Tim's projects: the Jerkatron, the Anti-G-Force Chair, and most important, Vincent Van Go-Go. The latter takes up almost all the space in an anteroom—big, but it doesn't look like your stereotype of a robot. Vincent Van Go-Go is a wooden board adorned with pulley-operated paintbrush, a canvas, and cans of paint attached to it, all of it hooked up to a computer. This robot paints pictures—really ugly ones like you made in seventh grade when you were stoned, with blots of color sliding off to one side, oranges and purples mixed at random. Tim slept underneath this robot/lean-to for several years. Recently, he moved into an apartment that he shares with some grad students. But even with the rent paid, Tim finds it hard to leave the womb-like techno comfort provided by his own creation.

Can you describe the robot you lived inside?

It's a plywood pup tent with a computer—controlled paintbrush hung over it with control wires. Sort of a big easel.

So where did you sleep?

Behind the canvas of this robot painting machine.

How long did you sleep in the robot?

A few years. I still do sometimes.

What about when you brought dates home?

Mostly, if they weren't scared away by my demeanor, then they were into anything weird.

So it helped out with the ladies?

Well, at first they liked it because it was weird, but then they didn't like it because it wasn't comfortable. So after the relationship had progressed, they pretty much didn't want to sleep in the robot anymore.

Why did you choose to sleep there?

Because it was comforting. Its like being in a box.

And it hid your sleeping from the [university] authorities, right?

The authorities don't care. I don't even know who they are.

But still, you couldn't have a bed out in the open, could you?

Oh yeah, I could. There were other people who had beds here.

So it wasn't about hiding?

No, it was more that my style of interior decoration tends toward the industrial.

TIM SITS IN A CHAIR HE MADE BY CUTTING APART AND WELDING A SHOPPING CART.

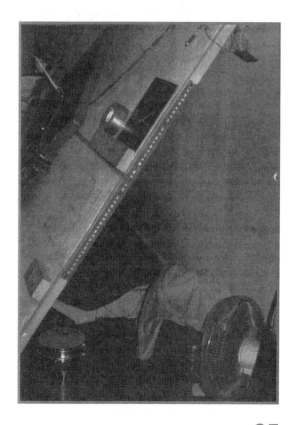

INSIDE THE ROBOT, BAD PICTURE, BUT YOU CAN JUST MAKE OUT SHEETS, AFRICAN DRUM, FAN, AND OTHER SLEEPING EQUIPMENT.

Entertaining Idea for People Who Live Inside Robots

and Houses, Too

It's a potluck! It's a swap meet! Everyone comes away a winner! Tell your friends to bring everything in their house they no longer want or need: food that's about to go bad, electrical equipment they can't fix, clothes they can't wear, junk they don't have room for, books they want to purge from their collection. Have everybody dump their stuff in the middle of your floor. Watch the excitement as your very own homes turns into a Salvation Army! This party is a great ice-breaker. Nothing brings people together like wearing one another's stuff. The only problem is that when you wake up the next morning, your place will look like a tornado hit it.

Why did you recently choose to move to a conventional apartment?

I don't know. I thought I'd try it out. I've slept there three or four times.

Why don't you like to sleep in an apartment?

I'd have to go there. All my toys are here. Everything I do when I'm awake is here, so I can work up to the last minute and then I can sleep.

I get it. Sleeping in the robot is about…

Convenience. Sleeping inside a robot is like sleeping anywhere else.

Now, vehicle dwelling—I did that too—that was also very convenient. This plethora of free parking spots in cities is the only free land. It's one of the major social programs. The government provides all these parking spaces and lets you use them for free. And there are a lot of people who live in vehicles, but they tend to try not to draw too much press because somebody may start an ordinance.

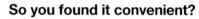

There don't seem to be a lot of ordinances, probably because the car takes up as much space with you in it as without.

So you found it convenient?

Yeah, I was working various temp jobs at the time. It was during some recession. I'd drive to work the night before when there was no traffic, I'd park and there was no trouble finding a parking spot, and then at 8:45, I'd climb out of the back of the pickup truck in my suit and go in and shoot the shit with the outer suit dwellers while the girls brought us coffee.

How did you keep as clean as everyone else?

I would just go over to a shower. A gym, or one of these [university] buildings. There are lots of buildings that have showers in them. There are all these things that are there, but if you don't look for them you don't know they're there.

Where are they now? *SFWP Reprint Edition.* Tim Anderson is still inventing and working to change the world. You can read about his projects and adventures (including spending a few days lost at sea!) at http://web.mit.edu/~robot/. Tim's goal is to be good to the Earth, instead of just trying to make cool technology. "Technology is mostly a substitution of capital for labor," he says, "and tends to result in more consumption of the earth's goodness instead of increasing that goodness."

Decor from the Dumpster

> *"There was no hesitance on the part of the soul-driven [Manson] girls to get down and grovel in the grunge of large bins of rotting animal and vegetable matter in order to sort out the good from the less good. The girls were into using their witchiness even in preparing for the daily garbage run when they would get a picture' in their minds as to what store would have the best…garbage."*
>
> —Ed Sanders, *The Family*

Above: Here's a kitchen cabinet set—with adorable 1950s details—being used as a garden center.

Right: With a little bit of chain, you can transform an old wok into a beautiful hanging planter.

Above left: A bulk peanut-butter container (free from a food co-op) can be used to store kitchen scraps before they go to the compost heap. This one has pared-down, classic lines. If the Gap made a compost holder, this would be it. *Above right:* High-fashion compost holder has a "punk" look. (It used to be a container for a fire-safety blanket.) This is the one to use when guests are coming for dinner.

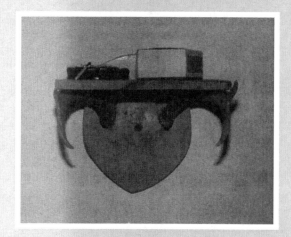

Above: Put an old cutting board on top of a pair of antlers, and presto! You've got a shelf.

Left: The rack that once held gum and candy at a news-stand becomes a bathroom "reading rack." The small shelves are the perfect size for zines.

Above left: Bathtubs are not just for virgins anymore. This one has a sink pedestal topped by a hurricane lamp, providing an eerie glow at night. *Above right:* Don't let that rainwater go to waste! This handy barrel collects "see-through gold" from the roof gutter and distributes it to the yard.

Left: These concrete "logs" come from an old gas fireplace. Placed in the garden, they have a second life as witty trompe l'oil.

Some friends of mine salvaged this handsome porcelain sink from the trash and installed it in place of a cheesy seventies unit. Beware: Older kitchen fixtures—sinks, cabinets, gas stoves—tend to take up a lot more room with their battleship-like beauty.

And, unfortunately, some antique drains require constant supervision to keep them from clogging. Next time your sink is slow to empty out, try this environmentally friendly alternative to Drano: squeeze the juice of one lemon down your drain and leave it overnight. In the morning, the clog will probably be gone!

Tips for small kitchens:
Hang everything from the ceiling

A decaying trophy animal hung above or beside your door makes a bold statement. It also helps to keep away the Jehovah's Witnesses.

Why Not Let THE MAN Plant a Tree for You?

Here's How One Fellow Did It

My friend and downstairs neighbor Marcus found out that you can get the city of Boston to plant a tree in front of your house—all you have to do is call the Parks Department. Or you can write a request to the City Aborist. I find it very comforting that Boston has a City Aborist. I've never seen him, but I imagine him wearing a tweed jacket, horn-rimmed glasses, and heavily creased pants. His hands would be speckled with freckles, and he'd jump in a startled way whenever the phone rings. I think he much prefers to get letters.

Well, anyway, a couple of years ago, Marcus wrote to request a tree be planted in front of our duplex. Months later, a crew appeared, tore up the sidewalk with jackhammers, and put a pathetic-looking sapling into the ground. So Marcus fired off another letter, asking for a tree on the other side of the house. Many, many months later, the crew showed up and deposited yet another sapling. Marcus recently asked for a tree on the corner and got an okay. We're expecting the sapling anytime now. Marcus plans to keep on requesting trees until the jig is up.

We find it hard to believe that the Powers That Be haven't caught on. After all, our house is small, and with the addition of the third tree, our modest strip of sidewalk will look like a rain forest. Or—who knows?—maybe every citizen is entitled to an unlimited supply of trees.

So check with your city's Public Works or Parks Departments to see whether you're eligible.

Marcus tending to the wild-flowers he's planted around Tree Number 1. The little fence is made out of pieces of scrap metal from the trash.

Tree Number 2.

Marcus at the proposed site of Tree Number 3. It will be about twenty-five feet away from Tree Number 1 and fifteen feet away from Tree Number 2.

SAMPLE LETTER

Dear City Arborist:

I'm writing to request that you plant a tree in front of my house when you do your planting this spring. It would be nice if you would plant it at [exact location.]. I've spoken with the owners of the house and they have given their okay.

Sincerely,
[You, the proud new proprietor of a tree]

Standing on a ladder to commune with Tree Number 1 in a photo with very poor contrast.

Where are they now? *SFWP Reprint Edition.* This is still possible! Residents of Boston can visit this helpful site: www. cityofboston.gov/Parks/StreetTrees/seasonal.asp. Most other communities offer the same service (with varying degrees of bureaucracy) usually through the Department of Parks and Recreation but, occasionally, through the Department of Transportation or the Urban Forestry Administration. So get online and make your government work for you! Trees for everyone!

- Old trunk used as coffee table. Amnesty International sticker on side came free in the mail.

- Yard sale finds: *Munsters* lamp, tiki stuff, mannequin

- Skulls, feathers, and bones left over from eighties' modern primitive fad

- Futon sofa with sad, sagging futon that always has to be propped up. Tapestry cover to hide menstrual stains.

- Political poster from Marxist movement in obscure Third World country

- Paintings left by long-ago housemates

- Dead spider plant

- Dead Mac

- Ridiculously huge speakers

- Pump-style spring water dispenser

- Items to be recycled stuck in odd corners

- Paper lamps that have lost their shape and come to resemble giant cocoons

- Books on shelf: *The Portable Nietzsche*, *Fat Is a Feminist Issue*, *Chariots of the Gods*, *Hammer of the Gods*

THAT "GROUP HOUSE" LOOK

WORK IS A FOUR-LETTER WORD...

BUT, THEN, SO IS PLAY

Coming across a shelf full of hot-pink drinking glasses in Caldors, I'm delighted—until I turn one of them over and read the "Made in China" label. Then I realize that my one-dollar fling, my impulse buy, is someone else's slave-labor job. Most of us have grown up with the idea that it's our right as Americans to be able to buy this kind of cheap crap; all my life there has been a stream of Smurfs and plastic decoder rings and patent-leather coin purses passing through my hands, little luxuries that seemed to come from nowhere. But during the past several years these bubble-gum toys and plastic baubles have started to make me shudder: how obscene that prison laborers and children are forced to work twelve hours a day to slap together statues of frowning clowns.

Office-working Americans don't begin to suffer in the same way as people in Third World sweatshops. But still, our jobs can be just as meaningless. So many white-collar workers—the advertising executive and the telemarketer and the copy editor at a computer trade magazine (my old job)—don't really produce anything. We're forced to manufacture the intellectual equivalent of pink plastic glasses and sad clown statues.

I'm not sure what to do for the people who slave away in the factories of Mexico and China and the Philippines. Maybe the first step is to free ourselves from our own boring and meaningless jobs.

CAN YOU BUY TIME?

A Rant about Work, Capitalism, Quakers, and Freedom, Brought to You Exclusively by the Editors Here at *Pagan Kennedy's Living.*

TIME IS MONEY.

I was about seven years old when I read those words on a paper garment bag my father had just picked up from the dry cleaner. I sat in the backseat of the car puzzling over the phrase. How could time be money? Was there some sort of coin I had never heard of, a coin made out of seconds or minutes?

"Dad?" I said, sticking my head in the crack between the two front seats of the car. "Dad? It says on the bag for your suit that time is money."

"That's right," he said. And then my father the economist explained the principle of cost-benefit analysis to me. "If I take my suits to the dry cleaner, then I save time, because I don't have to wash them myself. And that means I have more time to work at my office. I can make more money when I'm at my job than I could save by washing the clothes myself. So I take my suits to the dry cleaners."

"Is that why you go to work?" I asked him. "Just to make money?" For some reason this had never occurred to me before. I thought my father had to work because the fate of the entire planet depended on him—he was like Superman. Partly I'd gotten this idea from TV and partly I'd gotten the idea from my father himself, who disappeared while I was having breakfast and returned after I'd gone to sleep. He was always off somewhere, carrying out duties he couldn't quite explain to me.

"Why is there a number seven on the inside of your glasses?" I asked him once.

"Because I'm double-O seven. I'm James Bond. Now you've found out my secret identity."

I've seen few people so in love with their work as my father, he with his collection of legal pads and sharpened pencils, his briefcase that could only be unlocked if you knew the right combination. I find it strange, then, that he should have so enthusiastically espoused the idea that time is money. For that equation reduces work to nothing but its dollar value—when, in fact, our jobs are so much more. Making something, helping other people, taking on a professional role, mastering a skill—these qualities of work are essential to our dignity. Yet, we Americans have become so alienated from our own work that we often define ourselves by how much we make rather than what we do.

In the late eighteen hundreds, factories began organizing laborers into assembly lines, an innovation that marked a certain kind of conquest over time— over its consecutiveness, its this-has-to-follow-that flow. One person performs a task in a concerto of action, a process with a beginning, middle, and end. The assembly line turned workers into skipping records, each responsible for only a few seconds of that concerto. Such repetition transformed time into something entirely new, a series of units that could be stacked up like coins. Since then, almost all workplaces have become factories of some sort or another. A friend of mine reports that he worked for years at a copy shop that suddenly went through a corporate face-lift. Where once he'd been pretty much allowed to do the job in his own way, he now had to follow a script whenever he picked up the phone or when he took a customer's order. Where workers once had played whatever music they liked, they now had to listen to songs piped in from some central office. One day, the CD in the central office skipped for three hours, and the workers— unable to turn off the sound or communicate with the corporate deejay—had to endure the factory-like cadence of a few seconds of music, repeated over and over.

If time is money, then a number of disturbing conclusions follow. One is that we have power over death— for if we can trade our hours for dollars, shouldn't we be able to do the reverse? Shouldn't we be able to pay eight dollars or ten dollars, or whatever our time is worth, to secure another hour of life? The way we work encourages this alienation from our own death.

If time is money, then people cannot be equals. An hour of Bill Gates's time, for instance, is much more valuable than one of my hours. Why, then, should Bill Gates have to wait in line behind me at the bank machine? After all, the lost productivity when I stand in line is—what?—a few dollars. But when Bill Gates stands in line, society is losing thousands of dollars. Here's a modest solution, then: Everyone who makes more than five hundred thousand a year could wear a special button. Those people would be allowed to cut ahead in line. Traffic would have to screech to a halt so that they could cross the street whenever they needed to. Waiters would rush over to fill their orders. In such a utopia, the high earners would slide through life like greased pigs, never hindered by the friction of routine errands and ordinary delays. They would become perfectly productive.

In fact, this utopia is upon us. The rich ride over our heads in helicopters; they have their sushi delivered; personal trainers care for their bodies. Nowadays when you call information, a recording says, "The number you requested can be automatically dialed for an additional charge of thirty-five cents"—if you're willing to pay, you can even save yourself the trouble of dialing a phone number.

And if time is money, then our relationship to our work is robbed of its meaning. When you are paid by the hour, you aren't doing a project—like painting a sign, cooking a meal, building a fence—so much as you are doing time. In some offices, people have to "make work" just to fill up their eight-hour slots. Our workplaces are modeled after prisons.

The sad thing is, so many Americans want to stay in those prisons. We're impressed by stupid—even harmful—jobs, if they pay well. And we sneer at any activity that doesn't carry a cash value.

When I'm at a cocktail party and someone asks me what I do, I usually say, "Well, um, I'm a writer."

"Yes, but what do you *really* do," the person will ask.

"I'm a writer," I persist. "That's how I make my living. I swear."

"Oooh," the person will say, brightening. "That's great. Really impressive. You make money at it, huh?" And I can see that I've suddenly turned into a real writer in his or her eyes.

Moments like these, I'm overcome by a sort of existential nausea—not the French existential nausea, a sense of meaningless that is as flavorful as a crumbling cake of cheese, a meaninglessness that reeks of so many things: rain, wine, cigarettes, stale perfume. Instead, I'm possessed by the American brand of existential nausea, which leaves a taste in my mouth like a rancid Big Mac: There is no meaning but money. I am nothing but the sum of what I've earned.

So who came up with this strange idea that lies at the heart of our heartsickness, this idea that we are all for sale? It was Ben Franklin who coined the phrase *time is money*, and when I mention Franklin, you no doubt picture a portly man with a twinkle in his eye, flying a kite in the middle of a thunderstorm. That's how I picture him anyway, because that's how he appeared in my third-grade textbook. Forget the kite. Forget the knee socks. Forget the peculiarly delicate glasses stretched over that pudgy face. Picture this Franklin instead: the egomaniac who tells us that he sat down one day and "conceived the bold and arduous project of arriving at moral perfection." As surely as Franklin invented that little iron stove, he also invented the modern self—a self paved over in asphalt and open for business. If he aimed at moral perfection, he did so to fatten his wallet. "Nothing but money is sweeter than honey," he wrote in *Poor Richard's Almanac*. He believed that virtue is literally its own reward—an honest man becomes a rich man.

*   *   *   *

It never would have occurred to Franklin that one could work *too* hard or amass *too much* wealth. Indeed, he seemed incapable of understanding the dangers of America's emergent capitalist economy.

Not everyone was so naive. John Woolman, a contemporary of Franklin's and also a Quaker, was deeply disturbed about the ways in which people's time can be traded for money.

Like Franklin, John Woolman knew how to rake in the bucks. He'd earned a reputation as a reliable man, and this had been very good business at his fabric store. Unlike Franklin, Woolman decided that good business was a bad thing. He gave up his store, fearing that—if he became rich—he would no longer be able to live the simple life espoused by the Quaker faith. Woolman retired to raise his own food and do a little tailoring on the side; he also traveled around to speak out against slavery.

"[I] learned to be content with real conveniences that were not costly," he reported in his diary, "so that a way of life free from much entanglement appeared best for me, though the income might be small. I had several offers of business that appeared profitable, but I did not see my way clear to accept them, believing they would be attended with more outward care and cumber than was required me to engage in; I saw that a humble man, with the blessing of the Lord, might live on little and that where the heart was set

on greatness, success in business did not satisfy the craving." Woolman had a radical vision: an economy in which human life was not for sale. He took a stand against the slave trade, and he also took himself off the market—for Woolman believed that money makes slaves of all men.

In many ways, Woolman was the first slacker—he had a do-it-yourself aesthetic and a distaste for "care and cumber." While we may not be able to own our own farms and grow our own food anymore, we can live the simple life that Woolman espoused. If he were around today, I'm sure he'd be shopping at the Salvation Army, living in a group house, eating tofu and rice, getting around on a bike, flushing his toilet only once a day, and surviving on part-time temp work.

Capitalism is only evil if we make it so. We can refuse to participate in the so-called growth economy—an economy built on the destruction of the environment, the dismantling of communities, and the dehumanization of work. Rather, we can choose to exist within our own economy—one that honors balance and fairness. Like Woolman, we can decide that our time is too valuable to sell.

> Who came up with this strange idea that lies at the heart of our heartsickness, this idea that we are all for sale? It was Ben Franklin who coined the phrase *time is money.*

After a long, rambling introduction,
Meet a Santeria Priest

Though Steve Quintana has become a leader in an Afro-Cuban religion, he's vowed not to quit his day job

Back when I lived in New York, I got used to walking past botanicas, those dime stores of the divine that sell everything from candles in the shape of men and women, to good-luck floor washes, to money-attracting aerosol sprays. I knew that these stores catered to practitioners of a religion called Santeria, which was something like voodoo. Once in a while, I'd go in and buy a bag of powder or a candle, though I'd feel guilty for turning someone else's religion into my source for knick-knacks. Lately, I've noticed Santeria candles (glass cylinders full of wax with prayers and invocations printed on them) in stores all over the place, sold as decoration. It seems that urbanites have embraced the look of Santeria without understanding its substance.

Maybe I was guilty of that, too. But Santeria seemed to be everywhere I went, dogging me. When I visited Memphis, I found a wall full of magic potions sold in a five-and-dime store. There was something about the chintzy designs and the grandiose promises on the label; I had to know more.

When I read up on the subject, I discovered that the voodoo practiced down South, especially in New Orleans, is different from the Santeria that has taken hold in cities with large Hispanic populations. In New York alone, there's an estimated 300,000 followers. Like all the great religions, Santeria is a melting pot. When the Yoruba people were ripped from their West African homeland and deposited in Cuba, Trinidad,

and Brazil, they kept on worshiping their own gods. They were able to do so because the Spanish captors were more tolerant than the English who ruled North America; and also because the slaves came up with an ingenious method for disguising their gods. They put them in white face. For instance, the slaves transformed Elegba, god of crossroads and decisions, into the less-threatening Saint Anthony. This double-entendre religion flourished in Cuba, where whites also began to recognize the power of santero (priest) healers.

In recent decades, as Cubans have emigrated to the United States, Santeria has become a fixture in most of our large cities. Nonetheless, your average American doesn't know what the hell it is; mainstream culture hardly acknowledges the religion at all, except to malign it. In the '80s, a movie called *The Believers* portrayed Santeria as a cult, a bunch of psychos who sacrifice humans. In 1989, when a gang "sacrificed" a bunch of people in Matamoros, Mexico, the media immediately blamed the killings on the gang members' tenuous links to Santeria. In fact, their gruesome act should have been blamed on Hollywood, since it later came out that the killers may have repeatedly watched *The Believers*.

In the past few years, however, Santeria seems to have gained a new respectability. Many of the rituals involve animal sacrifice, which has made it vulnerable to legal attacks from the ASPCA and their ilk. But when a recent case went all the way to the Supreme Court, the ruling was in favor of Santeria's right to practice freedom of religion.

Santeria's gains have been more than just legal. Recent political and cultural trends have converged in its favor. The influx of illegal immigrants—and their persecution by our government—has probably helped Santeria; for it is not just a religion, but also a system of social support that caters to the poor. And, of course, Santeria is flamboyantly multicultural, which makes it uniquely suited to heal the deepest wound in our country: race.

Speaking of race, how can a white person with only a tourist's grasp of Spanish get involved in Santeria? Though I saw signs of the religion everywhere and hungered for its healing powers, it always seemed remote, part of a community I would never belong to. But that, too, seems to be changing.

A year ago, my friend Harvey mentioned that he'd been to a bembe, a sort of birthday party for one of the orishas (gods) of the religion. The bembe had celebrated Elegba, an orisha I had written about (under his Voodoo name, Legba) in a short story—the story had been oddly popular, appearing in four different books. As I listened to Harvey, I had an eerie sense that fate was at work, that a doorway had finally opened into this other world I'd been glimpsing for ten years.

I begged Harvey to bring me to the next bembe. So, on a sunny fall afternoon, we drove to a mixed income neighborhood in Boston, carrying with us gifts of fruit and rum for Obatala, the orisha who would be celebrated that day. We walked into a trim, neatly kept house, where people milled about. One room had been set up as a shrine. An array of small percussion instruments lay on the floor, and worshipers approached these, ringing bells and shaking gourds as they said private prayers.

The gathering had the rhythm of a party; the crowd began to mass in the living room; people kissed each other hello; there was chatting. And then something clicked, and Steve Quintana—the owner of the house and Boston's premiere santero—began a singing prayer. Drummers drummed; people

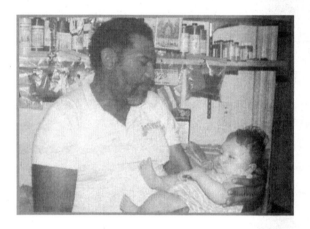

near, and we put out our hands to keep her in the center of the circle. The woman danced in a crouch, with her hands behind her, as if she were trying to hold something on her back. I recognized this as the dance of possession. One of the orishas was occupying her body. I tried to watch what happened to her, but the crowd closed around me; then I saw her hugging a friend. Later another woman became possessed, though in an entirely different manner. She began flailing about, speaking in tongues. "*A la cocina. A la cocina*," Steve called, and the woman was hustled away from the dance floor and out to the kitchen. The person standing next to me explained that the woman had been inhabited by the spirit of a dead person rather than a god—a lowly sort of possession that was not considered to be worthy of the crowd's attention.

The crowd. A gorgeous mix of skin colors and ages, holders of degrees from beauty school and from Harvard, people who boogied with ease and people who were shy of the dance floor. I'd been somewhat afraid that my pale, freckled skin would mark me as an outsider, but no, not at all. Here, a Latin openness and warmth ruled, making it easy to talk to strangers. People touched easily, exchanged glances as they sang. When I left that day, it was with a sense that I'd witnessed something extraordinary. I'd seen a woman inhabited by a god, but for some reason that seemed less impressive than the crowd itself: the miracle of different classes and races and nationalities mixing easily, our identities dropping away until we became a single singing mouth.

Needless to say, I was curious about Steve Quintana, the man who had masterminded this gathering. Harvey told me that Steve left Cuba in his teens to move to New York, and came up to Boston in 1987;

sang along. Soon the prayer session erupted into an all-out fiesta, with percussion, chanting, and ecstatic dancing.

A black woman in a purple dress began swaying in a woozy way. She bumped against those of us standing

since then, Steve had established himself as a leader in the Afro-Cuban community, in the media, and in the medical world. He'd tried to combat the negative stereotyping of Santeria by appearing on radio and TV talk shows; he'd also lectured to medical students at Harvard, MIT, and U. Mass about Santeria healing.

I was intimidated by all these accomplishments. And let me admit it: I, too, had been prejudiced by the media's stereotyping of voodoo and Santeria. I was a wee bit afraid of Steve because of his power—the power to invoke and communicate with gods. You wouldn't want to get on this guy's bad side.

But when I called up to ask him for an interview, Steve was gracious and avuncular. "Sure you can come by and talk to me," he said, implying that he was flattered. When I arrived at his house, he ushered me into his office—or, rather, one of his offices. This one was filled with botanica items, candles and powders and pictures of saints. Upstairs, he has another office, out of which he runs his graphics studio. For in addition to being santero, spokesman, and civic leader, Steve is a working artist: his illustrations appear on album covers and posters for Afro-Cuban bands.

I'd expected to find him—a representative of this religion so different from the staid Episcopalianism I grew up with—to be foreign. I expected a bent to his mind much different than my own. But as I listened to him talk, I was struck by a sense of familiarity. There is something about Steve's intelligence that is uniquely American. He's pragmatic, a do-it-yourselfer, a jack-of-all-trades. Though he believes in community, this man is a maverick whose real passion seems to be the invention of his own life.

A note on the interview: Steve talked in long-winded, far-ranging riffs that made perfect sense when I was sitting in front of him, but that were hard to render on the page. For this reason, I've rearranged what he said, organizing everything by topic.

On the growth of Santeria:
There are three to four million who practice Santeria. When I came to this country, you could count on your hands the number of Santerias in New York. There was no such thing as [Santeria in] Miami, Chicago, Washington.

Why [has it grown so fast]? Because of necessity. A doctor will charge maybe even five hundred dollars for a checkup and tests. If you come over to us—we offer spiritual cures. Even the [Catholic] church no longer gives that. They no longer visit the followers. We no longer see priests in peoples' houses. They've lost touch.

On Santeria's relationship to other religions:
We appreciate the saints of Christianity and everything that the Spanish brought [to Cuba]. I was even an alter boy. I was educated in church; my parents were Catholics.

The Vietnamese situation is similar to the Cubans'. [The Vietnamese] go to church on Sundays, but they also believe in Buddhism. If you walk into a store, you'll find a Buddha sitting there. They have both.

Incense used to be made for churches. Now it's made for botanicas and Santeros. It's also made for the Buddhists. Now you'll find candles in the supermarket. What the heck are candles doing in the supermarket? It used to be that Jewish people had candles in their own stores. Now you find candles all over the place, with the star of David in them. And we use [the star of David candles] too. Santeria has become a culture of cultures.

On healing:

Right now, I'm working with a doctor. I'm sending the child—well, he's not a child, he's twenty-two or twenty-three—this kid has lost his mind. I think he lost it because there was a spiritual power that was working on him. So I sent him to a psychologist and they sent him to a hospital and gave him pills. But now the doctor is talking to us and wanting to know what we found. That is very smart. If every doctor knew everything there is to know about sickness, people would not need a black doctor, or a santero, or a spiritualist.

[But for a lot of doctors, I'm a threat.] The figure this cockamamy person is out there with his house.... Well, I don't care much about what they think. If they don't think what we do is positive, then they don't care about their patients. And if they can't even compete with a group that's not even recognized....

Number one, the herbs we use are the same things used in pills. Second, we believe the herb has a lot more use, because we believe in the spiritual part. [The doctors] only use them on the basis of the chemistry. There are a lot of religions of the earth that practice herbal cures.

If you don't study such things, you're closing your eyes to the sun. That's the reason, I talk to [the media]. And now the Internet is opening this to a lot of people.

[Note: The Net may be the best place to start if you're interested in learning more about this religion. Just plug the word Santeria or orisha into your favorite search engine.]

On bad press and politics:

When the situation happened in Matamoros [Mexico], right away the papers were talking about Santeria.

And I was practically the only one talking against [the misinformation in the press]. We're not a Satanic group. We do more right than wrong in this religion.

In the movie *The Believers.*, they mixed up Santeria with a cult that was killing children. That's why we need to be organized. The Jewish organization has a group to defend itself against any slang or anything that is called anti-Semitism. And we don't even have a small group registered in Washington as a nonprofit to talk about the proper way to practice this religion. Someone's going to have to do it. If it's me, it'll be me.

Already the Supreme Court has decided that if sacrifices are part of the religion, then that's our freedom of religion. We won that. The ASPCA will continue fighting us, because you are not going to do a sacrifice in an apartment. We have to look for an appropriate place to do it. We're not like one of those American organizations that have lawyers and people who help out.

We're small-time and poor. Ninety percent of the people who brought this religion to the United States are Cubans. Five percent are Brazilians and from the Caribbean. The other five percent are from Africa. The closest [affiliate we have] is the Indian Nations of the United States. The cultivation of art and ideas and living out of the ground—our religion is the same. It comes from the beginning of the earth. People say we kill chickens. But the killing of an animal for the orishas, that is not a killing. That's an offering.

The government wants to know the good, the bad, and the ugly of this religion. We have a lot of mismanagement of this religion, people who abuse it. If we were organized and legal, we could practice more legally and more safely.

For example, the herbs [we use]. It's like a doctor. He wouldn't take a medicine and try it out on a patient

unless that medicine was accepted and legalized. We cannot talk about legality. We don't have a charter. We don't have a church. We don't have an organization. We are the only strong religion that is not registered. The Supreme Court legalized [animal sacrifice], but still we have the ASPCA come in and say "What are you doing with these animals?"

A lot of people hide [their ties to Santeria] because they're old-fashioned and they feel this religion shouldn't be publicized. I'm more Americanized. I was brought here when I was eighteen. I was not even in Santeria when I came in. I was lucky to find a high and respected priest at a house where I was introduced to this religion. I'm still learning a lot. What I practice, I know; what I don't know, I don't touch.

On making a living:

How do I make a living? I had my graphic design business before I was ordained as a priest in 1982.

I don't think I should make a living with my religion. That's one thing I complain about. A lot of people use religion as a business. The [Catholic] church is losing a lot of ground for that reason. The churches are closed a lot of the time. I remember when I used to go to church—I could go every morning. No longer. Now the church is locked.

In this religion, they call me at three o'clock in the morning and say, "Oh, my son is in jail."

I say, "Let me see what I can do." I go downstairs, do some prayers to make sure this kid can go early in the morning to see a judge.

If they have a problem, they come to me first, before they see a psychiatrist, a hospital, or even a lawyer. That gives me a tremendous responsibility to do right. [Many of the people who seek help] don't have green cards. They can't go anywhere. They can't go to the police if someone is abusing them.

I used to run a botanica. I tried to open a business, but no banks would give us money. So I'm back in the house, and I'm building up my studio again. My clients in graphics are the entertainment people. Since the sixties I've been one of the artists for Hispanic and black entertainment in New York. The concerts in Madison Square Garden, the Manhattan Center, the movies—I've been one of the artists creating the designs.

This house cost me a lot of money. So every month it's a headache [to pay the mortgage]. But I feel myself a rich man, because I'm respected in the community.

Where are they now? *SFWP Reprint Edition.* Steve Quintana and the House of Obatala are going strong. Visit them online at www.houseofobatala.com.

How One 8-Track Collector

The totally responsive woman: the real you.

CSI We can help you self-improve

Created His Own Dream Job

Russ Forster has built his own 8-track media empire. He publishes a zine called 8-Track Mind; and in 1994 he toured the country with his film camera, visiting the homes of readers to ask them about 8-tracks, politics, art, and the difficulties of dealing with Salvation Army staffers. The result was a feature-length documentary called So Wrong They're Right.

How did you begin publishing your magazine?

Well, I was on tour with my band and I met these people in Cambridge [Massachusetts] who were doing all the same kinds of things my friends and I [in Detroit] were doing—having disco parties with 8-tracks. We were at the time having weekly disco bowling at a local alley that really didn't have any business before we started hanging out there. We'd bring our 8-track players and bowl and dance. What these people [in Cambridge] were talking about was so similar.

Actually, I first found out that all these people were into 8-tracks because, when I came into town, I asked where the local thrift shop was and then I went barreling over to get 8-tracks and there were about three or four people all going through the 8-tracks and we were all having friendly competition.

So then you started your magazine?

I wanted to set up lines of communication across the country, because I had this idea that there were little pockets of 8-track activity in lots of different places and this might be a good way to get people in touch with one another and make it a cross-country phenomenon. It seems like the 8-track collectors have banded together and formed this network that's very caring. It's an attempt to form a community out of people who aren't in the same area.

I have noticed that a lot of people build friendships by writing in to the magazine and finding a kindred spirit who lives near where they live—or who lives in a completely different area, like in the case of Christine. She took a hankering to Abigail and built her up as this life idol and is proceeding to imitate every step that Abigail ever went through. That's pretty extreme. I never expected the magazine to change someone's life

that drastically. It was almost frightening that it did that, because I don't take it that seriously. But I think there is a serious…I think people are looking for like minds.

The Internet is kind of the same deal. People are finding little cliques that they feel comfortable with.

So it's like a pan-national tribe or something? But the 8-track network is different from the Internet isn't it?

No, I think its similar. There's now an 8-track news group set up [alt.collecting.8-track-tapes], and the person who's in charge of that is getting in touch with all these people who were never even aware of the magazine. It's a different medium for getting the same thing accomplished, getting people together.

Russ, on tour to promote his movie, poses in front of my refrigerator.

To be honest, when I started the magazine I didn't think there'd be more than a hundred people who'd be interested. But it's really exploded beyond that. And now it's going outside the realm of people interested in 8-tracks. Now people are writing in and saying, I have no interest in 8-tracks but I have the same kind of sensibility as you people have. I go to thrift stores. It's the same basic idea.

So these people have a similar sensibility because they're also living off of society's dregs?

Yeah, the pejorative media term is *trash culture*. I don't look at it as trash though. I look at 8-tracks as the ugly duckling of the music world, and a lot of people who are into 8-tracks can identify with being ugly ducklings in a social framework. They feel like they were thrown out or misunderstood, so they identify with that technology. Those people are starved for others who feel the same way.

That's the thing about your film—you seem much less interested in the 8-tracks themselves than in the people. It seemed liked an excuse to snoop through their apartments and to get them to reveal intimate details of their lives.

I was definitely interested in the personalities. That's what has kept me interested in the magazine too—the depth of the personalities of the people involved. Everybody seems to come to 8-track from a different point of view. The personalities were what fascinated me, what made me realize this could be a film. If I was putting out some kind of music magazine and people were writing in and saying, "I think Nirvana is rad," I don't know whether I would have been so enthusiastic. Because I could know what that kind of person's life is like without filming it at all. But these people, I had no idea what their lives were like until I pulled up and set down the cameras and started filming.

What surprised you?

One of the biggest surprises was that girl, Christine, seventeen years old. I asked her questions that I thought were pretty simple, like "What do you like to do?" "What do you like to write about?" "What are you planning for your future." These questions became tortured, soul-revealing, incredible…. The questions were much deeper than I ever realized. It was kind of torturous because I thought I was putting her through hell just by asking her these questions.

But that's part of her personality that I hadn't seen, the tortured side, from what she'd written in the magazine. From the magazine I thought she was just a bohemian wannabe, stuff that I could identify with, that I might have written when I was a teenager.

None of it had much to do with 8-track. I could see she was writing about her own trials and tribulations growing up as a teen in Southern Nowhere, a place lacking an aesthetic she could identify with. With most of these people I knew bits and pieces about them…With [one of the people profiled in the movie], for instance, I didn't know the depth of his business in 8-tracks. I thought it was just kind of a joke. And when he'd write to me with ideas like, You should be putting out *8-Track Mind* monthly, I just thought this guy was a kook.

But when I saw the business he had going and heard some of the phone calls he was getting regarding 8-tracks, I realized this was not a goof. He was actually making a lot of money. And that's why he wanted a magazine—to push 8-tracks as a commodity.

I notice that these collector magazines can degenerate into people pricing products, stuff like that. But you seem to encourage loss-of-virginity stories and spiritual experiences that are only vaguely connected to 8-track.

Well, I'm interested in personality. I'm not interested in pricing. I could easily turn the thing into the *8-Track Goldmine,* and it's kind of a scary thing to realize you could do that. I could set prices for things. I could decide I've got five of Funkadelics *One Nation Under a Groove,* so I'm going to set the price of that at $200 so I can make a ton of money. I could probably do that just by printing in the magazine that the tape is worth $200. That's how the collector markets work. But that's just not my cup of tea.

And 8-tracks. It's just never going to be the kind of market that other collector markets are, no matter what anyone says.

Well, 8-tracks degenerate so quickly. The rubber rollers melt, even when you're not using them. The fact that they're so flimsy undermines the collector market.

Yes and no. It doesn't undermine a certain collector market—the people who aren't going to play the 8-tracks. Because for them it doesn't matter if the roller melts. But [the flimsiness of 8-tracks] is a constant source of frustration for people who write in to the magazine. They want to have music they can rely on and the 8-tracks keep snapping all the time. Most of them eventually have to figure out ways to fix them. That's a rite of passage.

Well, the thing is, if you listen to your 8-tracks and enjoy them, you have to have a Zen attitude. If you use them, they're not going to last. They can snap after twenty-five minutes in the tape machine. Isn't that what keeps them pure?

I'm at the point where I know how to fix them so well that its second nature. I don't see that as a serious problem. But even knowing how to fix them, I realize that there are just a few 8-tracks that are going to get lost. You have to be willing to lose them. But I figure the risk is worth it.

You've become the most eminent personage in the 8-track field, haven't you?

People see me as a guru. I don't understand why. Sometimes I feel like I'm Chuck Woolery [of *Love Connection* fame], bringing these people together. I don't intend to create romances and friendships through the magazine. A lot of times I don't find out about it until I go out and meet somebody and they're talking about this other person I know from the magazine.

It's incredible to me how involved people are. They're sending in their life stories, with the intention of finding someone who's had similar experiences. It's almost like a singles club—not necessarily that people are looking for love in the pages of *8-Track Mind,* but they're looking for understanding, acceptance, community.

In the larger zine community, the zines that are the most interesting to me are the gay magazines. They're also an idea of trying to find people with similar attitudes and to create a community with a magazine, to communicate your own existence through the magazines. Music magazines don't communicate anything. I don't think they're creating any kind of community. I find them just boring.

So if you organized your 8-track pals into a political group and got them to march on Washington, what would they be marching for?

The 8-track community is looking for respect. There's

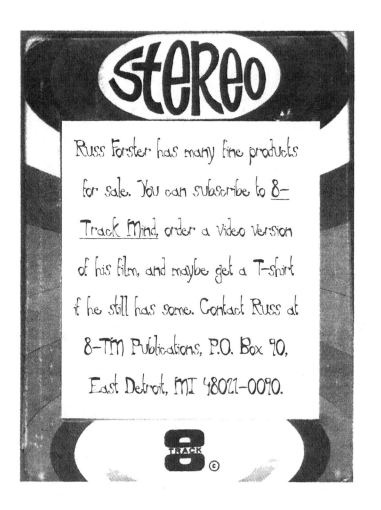

Russ Forster has many fine products for sale. You can subscribe to 8-Track Mind, order a video version of his film, and maybe get a T-shirt if he still has some. Contact Russ at 8-TM Publications, P.O. Box 90, East Detroit, MI 48021-0090.

a certain conspiracy theory behind this community in that it's rejecting the whole CD technology. On certain metaphorical levels, choosing 8-tracks is not choosing CDs. There's a political message there: We're not going to buy the stinking things you're telling us to buy. We're not going to believe the stinking lies you're telling us to believe.

And the lie about CD technology is a symbol for a larger lie, isn't it?

Yes—but the government isn't the source of the consternation. It's marketing; it's disposable culture. So we're creating a trash culture to go head-to-head with the disposable culture. This is a political act. We're saying, 'You're going to throw it away but we're going to fish it out of the garbage and find a way to use it, whether you like it or not."

Where are they now? *SFWP Reprint Edition.* Russ Forster is the man behind the website 8trackheaven.com. *8-Track Mind* ceased publication with issue #100 in January of 2001. Since then, Forster has revived the zine. Issue #101 came out in 2011, #102 in 2013, and #104 and #105 should be around by the time you read this.

WHERE IS SHE NOW?

A note from the publisher

I discovered Pagan Kennedy's writing in high school. We're both Marylanders—she's from Bethesda, I was born in DC into a family that fled to nearby Kensington. By the time I hit high school, Pagan's base was in Massachusetts, but her Bethesda roots guaranteed a presence for her zany zine, *Pagan's Head*, in the local head shops and groovy bookstores.

Back then, Bethesda was a different town. There were only a few tall buildings. Everything seemed smaller, quieter, more interesting, more varied. Almost a decade before DC's suburbs began to urbanize and reach for the sky with high-priced condo buildings, Pagan warned about gentrification in "House Hunt," featured in this volume. That gentrification has now obliterated the Bethesda of my youth (and Pagan's).

But there, in old Bethesda, at the end of the strange 1980s, I stepped into a cluttered, dusty head shop one day and bought a pair of purple-tinted John Lennon glasses, as one does, and went to pay for them. Scattered on the counter was an array of zines—including an issue of *Pagan's Head* just screaming for me to pick it up. It was free, anyway, so what the hell?

It only took a few pages for my life to change forever. *Pagan's Head* was my gateway to zine culture and, soon, I was trawling record stores, comic book stores, and anywhere else zines were available throughout the DC metropolitan area. I even started subscribing to some of them. A troubled teenager with a deeply disturbed family, I was an introverted ball of unexpressed anger until zines opened my eyes. Here were voices—some comic, some tragic, some insane—calling out in the wilderness. They told me: *It's okay to let it out. It's okay to express yourself. It's healthy to be outraged and say so.*

Zines inspired me to write, and eventually to publish. To gather up other, similar voices and give them a forum to express their vision.

By 1995, Pagan was known as the "Zine Queen," and she collected every one of her issues into one book, *Zine: How I Spent Six Years of My Life in the Underground and Finally...Found Myself...I Think*, published by St. Martin's Press. SFWP reprinted the book in 2014. The book you are now holding followed shortly afterward, in 1997, also through St. Martin's. It is very much a companion piece to *Zine*, and I always imagined *Living* to be a sort of outtakes collection from Pagan's zine years. *Living* first hit the shelves when I graduated from college, my first step in becoming a maturing hipster. Unlike *Zine*, *Living* offered a cohesive theme to live by. It felt like a call to action.

Looking back, I see her interviews with various people who were trying to change the world as a sort of bridge from her days as a zine queen to the Pagan we know and love today. While her fiction is excellent—and I encourage you to check out her three novels (*Exes, Spinsters,* and *Confessions of a Memory Eater*)—Pagan entered the 21st century primarily as a voice of creative nonfiction, writing for *The Boston Globe* and dozens of magazines and newspapers. Her nonfiction career earned her a Knight Science Journalism fellowship at MIT, grants from the Massachusetts Cultural Council and the Smithsonian, and landed her a gig as the design columnist for the *New York Times Magazine.*

I describe her as a "participatory journalist." Pagan isn't afraid to sit in at a swingers party (as an observer!), or to ride into the wilderness with a gun nut, or even to have a chip implanted in her brain for a story. Though she has interviewed folks who are strange and bizarre, her first love has always been to seek out the fringe adventurers, innovators, inventors, and entrepreneurs—all people who care about the world they live in and want to make it better for everyone.

We collected her essays about these fringe world-changers in *The Dangerous Joy of Dr. Sex* in 2008, and in *Inventology,* her 2016 book from Houghton Mifflin Harcourt, Pagan profiles the inventors behind some of the everyday objects we use, and describes how their inventions came about.

Pagan's exploration of these transformative individuals sometimes moves into the historical. In *Black Livingstone,* she crafted one of the few biographies of William Sheppard—a 19th Century African-American explorer and missionary who, almost single-handedly, broke the sadistic and violent yoke of colonialism on the Belgian Congo, then returned to die in near obscurity in an America crippled by Jim Crow. In *The First Man-Made Man,* she gave us a fascinating look at Michael Dillon, the first successful female-to-male sex change patient in the 1940s. In the opening essay for *The Dangerous Joy of Dr. Sex,* Pagan sits with the son of Alex Comfort, who was the troubled and strange author of *The Joy of Sex.*

It's been twenty-five years since I picked up that issue of *Pagan's Head,* and yet Pagan remains one of the most influential authors in my life. I hope this reprint speaks to a new generation of fans as well as those of us who have followed Pagan's journey through the years.

Learn more about our efforts to re-publish all of Pagan's out of print titles at www.pagankennedyproject.com, and see what Pagan is up to at www.pagankennedy.net.

Andrew Gifford
Bethesda, MD
October, 2015

The Pagan Kennedy Project

The Santa Fe Writers Project (www.sfwp.com) presents reprints of Pagan Kennedy's entire back catalog. See how the Queen of the Zines and the author of *Inventology* got started!

Zine: How I Spent Six Years of My Life in the Underground and Finally... Found Myself...I Think

Between the ages of 25 and 31, Kennedy published her own personal fanzine, *Pagan's Head*. Why? "To procrastinate, to trick people into liking me, to get dates, to turn myself into a star, and to transform my boring life into an epic story. And the scary thing was, it worked."

Pagan Kennedy's Living: A Handbook for Maturing Hipsters

In articles and cartoons that address the difficulty of staying hip in the '90s, Pagan provides a welcome alternative to *People* magazine and the later works of Hegel. Cruise through this book only if you want a extremely entertaining read and the opportunity to develop an unhealthy fixation on the fabulous Ms. Kennedy.

Platforms: A Microwaved Cultural Chronicle of the 1970's

In this hilarious, highly personalized popular history of what may be the goofiest of modern decades, pop culture critic and fiction writer Kennedy offers her insightful version of "guerrilla nostalgia."

The Dangerous Joy of Dr. Sex and Other True Stories

Nonfiction is the new black comedy in this hilarious collection of award-winning literary essays written by the infamous Pagan Kennedy.

Black Livingstone

The largely untold story of William Sheppard, a 19th-century African American who, for more than 20 years, defied segregation and operated a mission run by black Americans in the Belgian Congo. This stirring work tells how he eventually helped to break Belgium's ruthless colonial hold on the Congo.

Find out more at **pagankennedyproject.com**!